The Little Grownup:
a nostalgic Michigan boyhood

The Little Grownup:
a nostalgic Michigan boyhood

by

Hans G. Borger

Lulu Publishing

copyright 2007 by Hans G. Borger
All rights reserved

ISBN 978-0-6151-8580-4

Printed in the United States of America
First printing: December 2007

To the memory of my grandparents,
John and Martha Margetich,
whose kindness and love
set an example for me
that I very much appreciate and treasure

Contents

Introduction   1

Chapter One: Journey Back in Time   5

Chapter Two: I Was Born "The Little Grownup"   9

Chapter Three: A Child Model or a Model Child?   17

Chapter Four: Creepy Basements   25

Chapter Five: Flying Feet and a Squeezebox   37

Chapter Six: Soap on a Rope and Ricky Ricardo   45

Chapter Seven: Wildwood Days   53

Chapter Eight: The Balloon Room
and Bitter Lemon   61

Chapter Nine: Lightning Bolt
and Thunder Cloud   75

Chapter Ten: Trains, Planes
and a Cello   87

Chapter Eleven: Steak, Bear Meat
and Liver   103

Chapter Twelve: Goodbye City Life   121

INTRODUCTION

The 1960s and 1970s don't seem like that long ago. But looking at today's hyper-charged childhoods, complete with cell phones, computers, and other electronic wizardry, those years seem like ancient history. Even with all the technological advances, I don't think we've progressed. The doors of my school weren't locked for fear of a gunman. We knew our neighbors. We enjoyed going outside and exploring. We rode our bicycles without a helmet. We fell off. No one panicked. It was part of growing up.

My childhood was a normal one. Normal to me anyway. Looking back at all the experiences I had and the love that was showered on me, I'm not sure every boy was that blessed. My mother and father and their parents were immigrants from Europe and they had pride for both their native country and the United States. They gave me the best of the "old country" and the new.

I hope you enjoy my reminiscing. So many interesting people have crossed my path and influenced me. Many of those mentioned in this book are no longer with us, but they are alive and very vivid in my memory. I want to share them with you.

Thanks to my sister Monika Jordan, for her help in coordinating the pictures. A thank-you to my wife Heike for her technical computer assistance and patience while I was undertaking this project. Thanks to my parents George and Irene Borger and to my Grandmother (a.k.a. Oma) Hildegard Borger for their love and story fodder. An affectionate nod of recognition goes to my Aunt Dorothy.

Car windshield view as we drive into our past

CHAPTER ONE
JOURNEY BACK IN TIME

We were headed back into our own history. We were driving into Detroit. "Do you think the house is still standing?" I asked my Aunt Dorothy. "We'll find out. I haven't been here in over thirty-five years," she said driving across town.

"Be careful driving down there, it's not safe," Oma, my German-born grandmother had told her daughter Dorothy before we left her home in the Detroit suburb of Novi. Oma hadn't felt safe in Detroit since the 1967 riots. Her view of the city forty or so years later came only from murder reports on the local evening newscasts. Detroit's image of the number one crime city in the United States was well known to Oma.

I had flown to the Detroit area from Florida to visit my ailing grandma. I say Detroit "area," as our family and relatives had long moved out of the city proper. We had first abandoned the city of Detroit for the suburbs of Southfield, Farmington Hills, and Troy in the early 1970s. I was becoming nostalgic as I saw Oma's health and mood deteriorating. My grandpa, Opa, was long gone as were my maternal grandparents. My mind wandered back to simpler times of growing up, first in Detroit, and then in the suburbs. I was curious as to what had become of the home I spent my first years in.

As Aunt Dorothy drove closer to our old street, Strathmoor, there were a few houses boarded up. "It should be right around here somewhere," she said, as we got closer to Fenkell. I first recognized the former home of our neighbor "Grandma" Wheeler. The big red house didn't look as big as I remembered it, but it was still there!
Then a few doors down I whipped out the camera to take a quick picture as Aunt Dorothy stopped the car for a minute. Our old home WAS still lived in and was in good shape. "Looks like they added a second story."

Aunt Dorothy then drove the short distance to nearby Sussex where my maternal grandparents had lived. I had many warm memories of this home. Many pictures had been snapped on that front porch through the years. "That must be the house," Aunt Dorothy said. I took a picture again. The shrubbery hadn't been pruned back in a long while. The porch was full of old newspapers and an old office chair sat forlorn near the road. Still, I could almost imagine peering through the front window and seeing Grandma and Grandpa smiling back.
I almost felt like knocking on the door to talk to the people who live there now. Would they be interested in knowing what happened in that house on Sussex over forty years ago? Hopefully they are creating some memorable moments there as well.

JOURNEY BACK IN TIME

Grandpa and Grandma's house on Sussex in its 1960s prime

Our Detroit tour continued as Aunt Dorothy drove toward Greenview, where she and Oma and Opa had lived. "Oh wow, the drugstore is still there, but the cleaners is a church now." "Oh, that was the big department store 'Federals'. Looks abandoned now." Garbage was strewn along the road, but Oma and Opa's old home was also still there. The front steps were caving in and the side of the house looked rather forgotten. What would Oma, an immaculate housekeeper and gardener, think?

Aunt Dorothy seemed to think the current owners changed the basement windows. I happily

THE LITTLE GROWNUP

conjured up images of a special Christmas Day past in that basement where an actual visit from Santa Claus had miraculously occurred -- while Grandpa had been co-incidentally -- and to me very inconspicuously-- absent.

Detroit and my life had changed a lot over the last 44 years. It was an amazing trip and somehow comforting to know the aging homes were worn for the wear but still around. The famous Thomas Wolfe wrote that you can't go home again. Maybe not. But the nostalgic journey of writing this book began that day, as I recalled memories made in those homes. The people who made them so special to me aren't living there anymore, but by reading these memoirs, my hope is you can almost picture them standing on the porch waiting for us to visit.

CHAPTER TWO
I WAS BORN "THE LITTLE GROWNUP"

I can't put a specific day or year on memories. Looking back, growing up seems more like a colorful collage of vignettes and I hope you enjoy the rainbow. I was born an adult. No one seems to believe me, especially those who were there when I was growing up. But I never really did feel like a child and couldn't understand why I was being treated like one.

It was January of 1964. President Lyndon Johnson was in the White House. Hello, Dolly! would soon open in New York City, the first Beatles LP was about to be released in the United States and Hans George Borger arrived at the modest home of his parents George and Irene on Strathmoor in Detroit.

The houses were so close you could see what the neighbor was having for dinner. In our case the neighbors could look into our kitchen/dining room. We could look into their living room from our kitchen. "Theirs" was Marion and Bill Pritchard, an older couple who were delightful. Maybe they really weren't that old, but as a little boy they seemed old. I called most of my parent's friends "aunt" or "uncle."

THE LITTLE GROWNUP

"Aunt" Marion had a dog named Mitzi. Since the Pritchards didn't have any kids, Mitzi got all the attention. When we would visit, Mitzi would bark and carry on as if she were jealous of me. She probably was, as she would invariably attack my skinny legs. I didn't care for Mitzi.

"Aunt" Marion collected all kinds of fragile figurines of dogs and dancing ballerinas, many of which were placed on top of her new color television set. She not only had the most modern TV set on the block, but also the most modern Christmas tree. It was pure white and featured a colored twirling pinwheel shining towards it, making it shimmer in various 1960s hues.

Her husband Bill was always making comments about how he was God's gift to women and embarrassing poor Marion. "Uncle" Bill wasn't God's gift to women, but "Aunt" Marion apparently got along with him. They danced to the music on "The Lawrence Welk Show" on television on Saturday nights, which my parents reported through window watching. I looked forward to a Christmas or birthday card from "Aunt" Marion written in her memorable scrawling handwriting addressed to "Master Borger." Sometimes a dollar would be tucked into the card.

On the other side of our house was a small home where the owners kept a pet monkey. I avoided that place. The monkey peed all over and the place stank. I often visited the monkey's neighbor, though. Two doors down from us was a huge red house where "Grandma" Wheeler and her daughter "Aunt" Ellen lived. I'm not sure why the grandma moniker was stuck on "Grandma" Wheeler, as she could also have been an "aunt". The Wheelers always had some delicious molasses cookies for me. They had one of the biggest

I WAS BORN "THE LITTLE GROWNUP"

Christmas trees on the block and had the most captivating bubble lights on them every year. I think I liked the bubbles lights better than "Aunt" Marion's colored spectacle. Once in a while a short visit to the Wheelers wouldn't be enough, so I'd pack my little suitcase, parade down the sidewalk with it, and spend the night with my adopted grandma, probably much to my parent's delight. "Be sure and come back soon, Hans!" "Grandma" Wheeler would say the next morning as I returned home. Incidentally, Pa says if Ma was out shopping and I was alone with him, he would cart me over to either "Aunt" Marion or "Grandma" Wheeler to change my diaper. Just the thought of having to do that dirty chore would give him the dry heaves.

To back up a bit, I don't know why I was given such a German name. Pa's name was George; his father's name was George. Ma didn't like the name George, but it was good enough to become my middle name. I can't say I really suffered with the name Hans, but it was a pain to have to constantly tell Americans how to say it. In case you don't know, it is pronounced "Hahns." If someone would pronounce it like the word "hands" I would point to my fingers and give them my stock answer: "These are hands. My name is Hans." Of course it didn't help that some American Hanses did indeed pronounce their name "hands." The Germans added insult to injury and it comes out "hunts." I sometimes felt like a ketchup heir! On top of that confusion Grandma and Grandpa and several others added an "I" to the end, which Germans mean as a loving endearment, so I became "huntsy." Oh brother!

My sister Monika had it difficult, too. Most Monikas in the United States are actually Monicas. My brother Kurt had it the easiest. I don't think that many Curts are around. Monika and Kurt weren't even born yet at this stage of the story, so at this point in the book this is all irrelevant! Incidentally, I got out of the Hans/Hands/Hunts pronunciation crisis the easy way and adopted the nickname Jeff when I got older! That is irrelevant, too. In my youth and for this book, I'm still Hands...I mean Hans!

Aunt Dorothy, Oma and Opa at my first birthday

I've always had a healthy fear of fire, perhaps since I almost burned our house down at a very young age. My parents didn't coddle me in their first floor bedroom. I had my own bed at a young age, upstairs in the attic. I have always had a very low tolerance for cold and an upper attic bedroom in Michigan wasn't exactly the warmest part of the house. A space heater kept the area toasty and since I thought it would be nice to have a warm luxurious pillow, I put the pillow in front of the space heater one evening before going to bed.

It wasn't long before smoke started filling the room and luckily the whole place didn't erupt in flames as my parents discovered my latest idea.

I WAS BORN " THE LITTLE GROWNUP"

Not long after that I recall an insurance salesman coming to the house and talking about fire insurance and how important it was. I just imagined any time the house would catch on fire.

I saw that the adults could get in some trouble with fire as well. Grandma had taken me with her to the A&P where she bought some frozen raspberries to put on top of the bread pudding she was making. We just had to bake it. She had an old gas stove and oven. She lit a match and hunched down as she tried to ignite the pilot light on the oven. Suddenly I heard a poof and saw a flame. Grandma had singed her hair and ran into the nearby bathroom and quickly held her hair under the faucet. The bread pudding was soon in the oven after she tried again successfully to light the oven. It tasted great with the hot raspberries on top, but I wonder if she hadn't had singed her hair if it would be as memorable an occasion?

The kitchen in Grandma's house on Sussex was tiny. Today we have kitchens that are huge and may look wonderful, but I can't imagine anything as tasty coming out of them. Grandma usually had something cooking in the "Guardian Service" iron cookware that was the mainstay of that little room. She was an excellent cook. One of our favorites was her German style potato pancakes. She would grate the potatoes by hand, which for an entire table full of hungry people could be a painful experience. Her secret ingredient was to add several shredded carrots to the recipe. If someone told her this wasn't the traditional way to make potato pancakes, she would reply, "These are more like health pancakes." With applesauce they were mouth watering.

THE LITTLE GROWNUP

Grandma in her kitchen

Grandpa along with Grandpa's mother, Kate who lived with Grandma and Grandpa, were Catholic. In those days Fridays meant no meat for Catholics. Apparently the pope also influenced Grandma, who was Lutheran, but also did the cooking. Every Friday night the menu never varied. Grandpa always demanded macaroni and cheese with tuna fish on the side. Ma says she had her fill of macaroni and cheese while growing up and she rarely made it for me when I was a boy.

Grandpa's mother did give Grandma some competition in the kitchen. She made some great stuffed cabbage or as she called them "sarma." "Baba," as we affectionately called her, was a typical old-fashioned great-grandmother. By the time I was born, she was already in her mid sixties. She was originally from a small town called Vrbova in what was then Yugoslavia, and like so many immigrants she found her way in her new homeland by using the talents she learned in the old country.

I WAS BORN "THE LITTLE BROWNUP"

Her family now gladly enjoyed her Croatian baking skills. Earlier she had worked in the Pervine Bakery on or near Livernois in Detroit. I have a picture probably taken in the 1940s with Baba and five co-workers working in the bakery. A huge mixer and several large mixing bowls are seen. It doesn't look like easy work.

I'm not sure what ever became of Grandpa's father. He never talked about him, so I assume Baba had to work and raise him alone. Baba crocheted and knitted everything, from sweaters to chair coverings to blankets. Her lace-like tablecloths were works of art.

I'm sure it must not have been easy for Grandma to have another woman living under the same roof with her. If this was ever a problem, I never heard about it. Baba was very loving, but this almost caused a kidnapping case to be reported. I had packed my little suitcase again and this time I was staying over at Grandma and Grandpa's house. In the middle of the night Grandma checked on me, but I wasn't in my bed. In a panic, Grandma checked everywhere, until she found me safely sleeping with Baba, who had apparently rescued me from my lonely bed to keep me warm beside her.

Baba had a couple of chihuahua dogs, Toolie and Tequita. These nasty beasts had a mean bark and liked to snap at me or most anyone else that tried to pet them. Eventually Toolie disappeared. I don't recall what happened to that evil ugly canine. Maybe Baba or Grandma or Grandpa realized two chihuahuas outnumbered one of me. Tequita stayed around awhile to plague me, but eventually she bit the dust.

THE LITTLE GROWNUP

Grandma, Tequita and me

Baba also had a cool pet parakeet named Mickey. Mickey was more my speed as he didn't bark or bite. He just stayed in his cage and looked at you. Baba taught him how to say "Martha is knitting Mickey a pair of pants" in Croation! One more thing about Baba. She liked to watch Perry Como sing on television. Baba had great taste. To this day, I am fond of listening to Mr. Como.

I recall our home on Strathmoor in Detroit, but don't remember too much of the day-to-day goings on of the early years. Almost burning the house down is of course etched into my mind. So is my misguided attempt to become some sort of acrobat. Somehow I decided it would be fun to stick my head through the wrought iron holes in the ornate posts that held up the front porch. Somehow I couldn't get my head out. Somehow neither could Ma and Pa. Somehow the City of Detroit Fire Department had to be summoned to get me out! Somehow I survived.

CHAPTER THREE
A CHILD MODEL OR A MODEL CHILD?

Ma and Pa were married at Holy Cross Lutheran Church in Detroit in 1962. Grandma and Ma attended Holy Cross. Ma had graduated from the Lutheran school system of Detroit. In those days people with a German background were either Lutheran or Catholic, mostly determined by where you had lived in Germany. Eventually Ma transferred to Pa's church, St. James Lutheran Church, and that is where I was baptized.

Oma, who was actually my step-grandmother, and Grandpa, who was actually my step-grandfather, were my godmother and godfather respectively. At my young age I didn't understand that they were not really blood relatives. It didn't matter. Oma and Grandpa were always very close to me and I felt a strong bond with them. It was a nice gesture by Ma and Pa to give their stepparents the responsibility of being godparents to their firstborn son.

As I mentioned, Grandpa and his mother Baba were both Catholics. That made for an interesting mix. I guess the Lutheran church didn't care that

THE LITTLE GROWNUP

Grandpa might try to slip his godson a rosary! I still have the church bulletin from the day Oma and Grandpa became my godparents. It was March 15, 1964. The announcements include an invitation for "those who work downtown" to hear Dr. Martin Luther King speak from 12:10 to 12:50pm at the Central Methodist Church.

beaming godparents Oma and Grandpa

I don't recall the early years of going to church. Pa relates the story that he was on the church board in those years. He found out that the church roof was leaking. He talked to the pastor and made arrangements for some roofers to fix the building before any more damage would be done. He bought a case of beer for the workers and put it near the altar. When the job was done, they would enjoy a beer. The pastor apparently had some words with Pa about not keeping the sanctuary holy. Pa didn't mince any words and defended his actions. Right or wrong, the roof was fixed and the church board was pleased. The workers must have enjoyed their beer as well.

A CHILD MODEL OR A MODEL CHILD?

Even though I feel like I was born The Little Grownup, I did have a lot to learn. Since my parents were bi-lingual, they naturally decided to teach me both English and German. Apparently this was too much for me to comprehend, as when I was with my little playmates, I couldn't understand why they didn't understand me when I spoke German. I cried. That was the end of a bilingual boy as far as my parents were concerned, so our household became 95 percent English speaking.

Soon I also made my first and last attempt at being a supermodel. Ma had my picture taken at the Montgomery Ward department store. I looked quite dapper in my little vest and bowtie. "Montgomery," as Oma called it, was a nationwide chain. The "Montgomery" folks liked my look and began displaying my picture to entice other parents to get their brats photographed.

*The Little Grownup
as a Montgomery Ward model*

THE LITTLE GROWNUP

Grandma seemed to get a kick out of buying clothes and dressing me in them and she did have fashion taste. Some of the many pictures taken at that time show me dressed in fancy suits that would rival any model. One Easter, my outfit made me look like a miniature mafia boss inspecting his Easter basket, complete with hat!

In June of 1966 my sister Monika Lynn was born. We got along very well as far as I recall. Oma later informed me however that I was so very jealous of Moni and that I tried to bite her toes off. I have no recollection of that! My recent vocabulary knowledge of baby talk came in handy as Ma and Pa sometimes couldn't understand Monika and used me as an effective translator. When I was in my upstairs bedroom, Moni would call me down to the first floor. Since she couldn't pronounce "Hans" I became "Hasa." Monika, or "my little sweet potato" as Grandpa called her, was a welcome addition to our growing family.

Ma and Pa with Monika and me

A CHILD MODEL OR A MODEL CHILD?

My love for music began at a very young age. I can picture Ma ironing in the front room of our house with her Magnavox stereo record player blaring. In the days long before CDs and Ipods, the modern way to hear music was through the phonograph record played on a stereo record player. Ma's stereo not only had a great sound, but it was a beautiful functional piece of dark wood furniture as well. The left side had a sliding door that revealed a record storage compartment. Opening the right side revealed an automatic record changer turntable with am/fm stereo.

Ma played German records as well as American standards of the day. My favorite album quickly became the soundtrack from the movie "The Sound of Music." The organ playing in the wedding song was simply majestic to my ears.

Soon I had my own little portable record player. It didn't have the tone of the Magnavox, but it was mine. "Grandma" Wheeler gave me a stack of children's records and I played them over and over. Ma gave me some of her old records from the 1950s. One of my favorites was pianist Liberace playing "Dark Eyes." The record was the size of a 45 single, but it played at 78 rpm. The label said it was "compliments of Herman Biscuit Company." Biscuit companies sure gave nice promotions away in those days! This Liberace song had a tempo that started out slowly and increased to a fever pace, just as the record spun quickly on the turntable. This was perfect to use as background music as Moni and I jumped up and down on our beds. Incidentally Pa didn't think jumping up and down on our beds was such a great idea. I never found out why.

I soon did learn that no one seemed to value their records as much as I did. To me, music

THE LITTLE GROWNUP

should have been playing all the time! Once in a while Oma and Opa played their record player. Oma always worried I would break it. I remember wanting a copy of their German band LP by Will Glahe. Oma didn't want to relinquish it, but she did give me some ancient 78s of Strauss waltzes, which transported me into the world of her ancestors.

The record cabinet of Grandma and Grandpa was my favorite. Their collection of albums, mostly from the 1950s, would mark me for life as a fan of that era. In fact, as most of my contemporaries were being influenced by the pop sounds of the early 1970s, I'd be found listening to the string orchestra of Percy Faith or the rousing big band sounds of Glenn Miller.
I loved looking at the fascinating album covers. Percy Faith had some beautiful women on his album covers. The pictures were almost as interesting as the big letters "COLUMBIA" on the red and black labels or the RCA Victor dog on the others. Some had pictures of exotic places I hoped to visit someday. The albums "Holiday in Vienna" or "Brazil!" let me dream of far off lands. The harmonies of the Four Lads or Doris Day captivated me.

These LPs are still treasured as a vital link to my youth as I can still picture Grandma and Grandpa's hi-fi in the corner of their front room on Sussex playing the same albums that are now cherished heirlooms. A tiny bit of Christmas with Grandma and Grandpa still returns every year with the sounds of their "Christmas in Zitherland" record by Ruth Welcome, played on that same treasured hi-fi now in the corner of my living room.

A CHILD MODEL OR A MODEL CHILD?

Glamorous Grandma and the hi-fi

In those days the milkman delivered milk and dairy products to our door. Twin Pines Dairy was the king at marketing to children. They sponsored a clown kiddie show on Detroit television for years. They offered school field trips to the plant to see how milk was put into cartons and how cottage cheese was made. Maybe they figured that if they built up their clientele at a young age, they would keep their loyalty later.

Grandpa's neighbor Jack McTague was a milkman for Twin Pines' rival Borden's Dairy. Jack had a round face and with the right make-up he could have been a Borden's TV clown. Unfortunately for Jack, Borden's didn't have a clown for a mascot. They had Elsie the Cow!

Jack was always giving me balloons with Elsie or other Borden's characters emblazoned on them. Once he even gave me an Elsie the Cow doll. It would probably be worth a small fortune to some collector today, but I didn't like her plastic horns so Elsie didn't stay with me very long.

THE LITTLE GROWNUP

In just a few years the milkman would be a relic of the past. I'm glad I got to be in on the tail end of this American icon.

*Baba and Grandma
with Lucy and Jack McTague*

CHAPTER FOUR
CREEPY BASEMENTS

Times were changing. In 1967 Detroit had some terrible rioting. Tension between Blacks and Whites was at an all time high. All of this was pretty much sheltered from me. All I recall of it was one of the neighbors on our porch telling me not to go too far away from home or the "boogie man" would get me. I certainly didn't want that to happen. My own world of "Aunt" Marion, "Uncle" Bill and the Wheelers was enough for me. My parents made the decision that seemed to be the norm White flight of the day. Plans were made to leave Detroit. Pa found a piece of property in the nearby suburb of Southfield. It had five acres. He wouldn't have to watch "Aunt" Marion through the window anymore.

The building of a new three-bedroom home began on the large lot on McAllister Street. Pa had been a carpenter for several years and even though someone else built the home, he designed and supervised its construction. There would be a large family room, front room, full basement, and plenty of property outside for his children to roam in.

THE LITTLE GROWNUP

About this time, in 1968, my brother Kurt Andrew came into the world so the Strathmoor house was getting too small anyway. We bid farewell to Strathmoor, the Pritchards and the Wheelers. I think the peeing monkey was dead by this time, so we didn't have to say goodbye to him. The rest of the family abandoned Detroit for the suburbs as well. Grandma and Grandpa soon moved to Farmington Hills and Oma and Opa and Aunt Dorothy left for the suburb of Troy, Michigan.

Our new house on McAllister featured a beautiful fireplace in the living room with a black slate mantel in front of it. The black slate wasn't fond of Moni's head as she rocked her rocking horse in front of it and promptly hit her head on it, sending her to the emergency room for stitches.
Monika had her own bedroom but I had to share a bedroom with Kurt. Ma and Pa turned their bedroom into the most stylish room of the house. Pa put in red shag carpeting about two feet up the sides of the walls. This idea must have been way ahead of its time as I have yet to hear of anyone else doing such a thing! I used to like to go in there and sit on the floor and read a book, my back and head leaning against the soft carpeting.
The house had a forced heating system with vents in every room. I never liked the cold Michigan winters and remember asking Ma to turn on the heat for just a few minutes extra before I had to go outside in the cold. I would curl up next to that vent and try to soak up just a few more degrees of heat before having to leave the comfort of the house.

The house on Strathmoor had a finished basement where my parents held parties. The

CREEPY BASEMENTS

fond memories of that room were history, as the basement in our new house was the scariest place on earth. Having to go down there alone evoked sheer terror, even with the lights on. The basement must have been built below the water table, as there was a visible hole in the corner. Once in a while, a loud sub pump would come on automatically to keep the water from flooding the basement. The shrill sound of the pump alone was enough to make a kid pee in his pants.

Of course if Ma was doing her laundry down there or if Pa was in his workshop, it was safe to visit. I would open the door of the big freezer down there and examine the packages of frozen meats, fruits and vegetables. I would open a plastic container and take out a couple of frozen cherries to sample. I would proceed to the big wooden barrel that Pa had filled with cabbage in what would become a futile attempt to make homemade sauerkraut.

The basement had a lot of other interesting things to explore. A cypress knee lamp on a shelf. Some old party hats with naked women pictured on the top. Sometimes Moni or Kurt could be enticed into the basement with me and we would climb into a huge wooden box where our old toys were stored.

Once Ma let us use the old electric stove in the basement. We were going to have our own restaurant and serve hot dogs. We made menus and invited Grandma to be our first customer. She couldn't come. We served each other.

On rare occasions we would lose electricity in the aftermath of a storm. The basement would turn into a lake as the sub pump couldn't work and water poured up through the hole. The basement also featured its own black telephone mounted on the wall. Why this extravaganza was planned is a

THE LITTLE GROWNUP

mystery, as the basement was not the hotbed of activity.

The creepiest basement belonged to Opa on the East Side. I was blessed to actually have three grandfathers. This Opa lived by himself in what was then known as East Detroit (thus the moniker "Opa on the East Side"). I was told that this man at one time was married to Grandma. I figured it was perfectly normal to have more than two grandpas. After all, I had plenty of "aunts" and "uncles."

Poor Opa on the East Side must have had a rough life. He not only was a German soldier in World War Two but didn't adjust well to his new life in the United States. Grandma divorced him. He was an alcoholic. Ma took us to visit him occasionally. She did his laundry. She made sure his bills got paid. His English made it hard for us to understand him or maybe it was his drinking that slurred his speech.

His house as mentioned featured a basement that was creepier than ours. Somehow I wasn't afraid to explore it though. It had a broken down drinking fountain in one corner, an old wringer washing machine in another. I'd handle some of the dusty red and green bottles in the bar, wondering what was inside them. Chards of glass covered the floor. At the far end of the main room was yet another small damp room. I was sure this was the dungeon where the prisoners must have been kept in the olden days. Opa on the East Side had several cats that had the run of the house and basement. Invariably a cat would jump out of nowhere at me during my basement exploration, sending me darting quickly back upstairs.

CREEPY BASEMENTS

It's kind of sad looking back at him now, but "Opa on the East Side" never really played much of a role in my childhood. He played the harmonica and maybe that was a link to me and my love for music. He was rather pitiful, spending a lot of his time after work in bars. He was rarely with us for holidays, so I don't really know how he spent them. He must have been quite lonely.

Soon it was time to start school. Southfield was a growing city and I would get to attend the brand new Eisenhower Elementary School. The teaching caliber was excellent and the school facilities were state of the art. I enjoyed learning. I enjoyed my new friends. I was bored. Pa said the teacher called him and said I kept answering all the questions she asked. I wouldn't give the other kids a chance to reply. My apparent reply: "Can I help it if they are too dumb to know the answer?" I couldn't help it that I was born The Little Grownup! Apparently Mister Smarty Pants didn't know everything after all and kept going to school.

Eisenhower was a great new world. The day would start with the school's public address system beeping, followed by the student of the week reading the events of the day and the school cafeteria menu list, which would almost always end in "condiments, bread, butter...and milk." Then the solemn announcement: "We will now stand and say the pledge."

I fell in love with that microphone when I was chosen student of the week and pretended I was a big important radio announcer like Detroit's famous radioman Dick Purtan. Ma had him tuned in every morning while we ate breakfast. He had the job I wanted. I beamed as the school secretary Mrs. Wieland showed me how to broadcast the important information about the fried chicken, vegetables, condiments, bread,

THE LITTLE GROWNUP

butter... and milk before leading the school in reciting the Pledge of Allegiance. "...With liberty and justice for all."

Eisenhower classrooms were built around a "commons" area. When we were collectively summoned into the "commons," we knew it would be special. Sometimes a film projector beckoned us into the world of nature compliments of Encyclopedia Britannica films. One of the teachers must have lived in Dearborn, since a lot of the movies started off with a Dearborn Public Library film leader.

Once in a while we saw a filmstrip, which was a kind of glorified still slide show accompanied by a cassette tape. We even got to watch the television show "Zoom" on the fledgling Public Broadcasting Service. Young minds were definitely given a workout. In gym class we did everything from throwing around the medicine ball to playing floor hockey. We made a piñata, painted pictures, and fired clay pottery in a kiln in art class. Music class provided an opportunity for us to sing American standards or play the xylophone.

Looking back at the "Dwight D. Eisenhower School Winter Program December 21, 1972," the provided music was as varied as the religious makeup of the students. The "Holiday Customs Around the World" theme featured me as soloist singing "O Christmas Tree" in German with six other pseudo German kids as backup singers. Southfield had a large Jewish community and us Christian kids sang alongside them about their dredyl custom. Jean O'Conner played the tambourine to a lively version of "It's Hanukkah!" while a few songs later we were back to Jesus and "Silent Night." "Jingle Bells" appeared twice on the program with my friend David playing Santa Claus in one of the versions. Whether Christian,

CREEPY BASEMENTS

Jewish, or just Santa believers, the parents beamed at seeing their children perform.

One year we learned the art of business as we brought in popcorn poppers and supplies from home and sold the popcorn to fellow students during recess. No one gave a thought that we might burn ourselves with the hot oil or that the health department didn't inspect the popcorn being sold. I think the profits from our sales purchased the seedling trees we then planted along the Eisenhower fence line.

I was terrified one summer to find out that the mean Mrs. Boychuck would be my teacher. The rumors were just meant to scare us. She became a favorite. She even held an after school yoga class which I attended. Elementary school aged children doing yoga was quite maverick in the 1970s. It probably still is!

Mr. Jeris read us the wonderful book "Charlie and the Chocolate Factory" out loud. Mrs. Gordon taught us the concept of direction using a ridiculously funny plastic man called "Mister O." Miss Cooper let us have a pet guinea pig in the classroom and inspired me to get one of my own.

Recess had us exploring the playground with its swing sets, monkey bars, and coveted crow's nest, which seemed to be everyone's favorite hideout but could only accommodate several students at a time.

The Eisenhower library became another favorite world of mine. Not only did it have books, but a collection of small films, which could be viewed on individual viewers. Long before videotape, this innovation really fascinated me. Especially the movie about friction, which showed a bar of soap flying out of the actor's hand. For some reason that one became one of my favorites.

THE LITTLE GROWNUP

We didn't have too much homework to do. Once we were studying fire safety and had to make an escape plan on a map and practice it. We also made a fire extinguisher for our kitchen. The fire extinguisher project was easy. It consisted of getting an old coffee can, making a special fire label for it, and filling it with baking soda. We were told throwing baking soda on a fire would put it out. We didn't test this, so I still don't know to this day if it is true. My fire safety plan was foolproof. Kurt and I shared a bedroom. If we suspected a fire, we would touch the doors to see if they were hot. If so, we would open our bedroom window and climb out. I wanted to test this to make sure we could do it and Kurt of course was very happy to participate. As we were climbing out the window, Pa walked in the door. "What are you doing? Get back in here right now! Have you lost your minds?" He couldn't believe that climbing out a window was a homework assignment.

I didn't bother to show him the handy dandy fire extinguisher. Of course in my mind I knew we had done the right thing. Remember, I had almost set my bedroom on fire years ago, but now I'd be ready if it happened again!

The school system also gave us a pretty good scare about smoking. They showed us filmstrip pictures about how a lung looked after smoking. It was scary stuff and I wanted to be able to breathe! Pa smoked. Grandpa smoked. Opa smoked. "Opa on the East Side" smoked. I felt we were doomed! Pa didn't want to hear anything about his smoking and could get rather angry if I kept bringing it up. In the car, in a restaurant, at home, he felt he could smoke wherever and whenever he wanted to. And he did. Years later he finally did give it up. I am very grateful that the

CREEPY BASEMENTS

Southfield schools did such a good job in educating us. Too bad the parents weren't included!

Sometimes Ma would take us mall shopping or to the grocery store with her. I guess especially during our school summer vacation she had no choice. Most of her grocery shopping was done at Great Scott! Supermarket on Eight Mile Road and Telegraph. Great Scott! (complete with exclamation point) might have been so named after the managers watched boys like me in their store.

One time Ma was buying tampons and while we were waiting in line I inquisitively asked, "What are those used for?" She didn't want to answer then and there, so of course I just got louder and louder until everyone around was staring at us. "Why won't you tell me what they are for? Is it a secret or something?" I said.

It is no secret that kidnapping and child safety were not problems when I was growing up. If we went to the Tel-Twelve Mall, we were able to walk around for a while by ourselves and meet Ma in a few minutes at an appointed spot. Once in K-Mart she didn't appear at the precise minute. Surely she didn't leave us alone? Kurt was getting ready to cry. Monika was anxious. I took action. Soon over the loudspeaker all of the customers heard "Irene Borger, your children are waiting for you at the customer service counter." When she arrived about ten seconds later, she was not amused. We usually got a frozen Coke at K-Mart. She didn't buy us one that day.

Invariably every year we would have a school field trip to Greenfield Village. Henry Ford put together this historical museum as he collected famous houses and buildings from all over the country and brought them to Dearborn. Little did we know how privileged we were to live so close to this American historical wonderland. I remember listening to Edison's voice on the first phonograph as he recorded the poem "Mary had a Little Lamb." The Wright Brothers bicycle shop was also quite memorable as was the home of American dictionary legend Daniel Webster.

The chair that President Abraham Lincoln was shot in was also on display in the Henry Ford Museum and a guide noted that several souvenir seekers had taken several strands of fabric out of the chair to take home with them. I wondered what they would do with something like that. On a subsequent trip I noticed that the chair had been encased in plastic.

The only souvenir I remember bringing home from a school field trip was when we visited a working farm somewhere in the Detroit area. They had a small country store gift shop. All I could afford was a small potpourri sachet, which I purchased and put in my underwear drawer. It smelled like cinnamon and cloves. I felt like quite the gentleman having something so unique.

I was probably the only one in my class who had a potpourri sachet, but everyone had to follow the fads of the day. Someone brought some "Pop Rocks" candy to school. These flavored sugar bits would crackle and pop in your mouth. Of course everyone had to have them and the party store near our house was immediately sold out of them. Their supply was quickly replenished when they saw the customer sales potential.

CREEPY BASEMENTS

Eisenhower Elementary School students also caused a run on "Wacky Packages." These stickers featured pictures of real brand named products with slightly altered names and packages. The "Neveready" assaulted battery boasted zero lives and the slogan "keeps you in the dark." A can of "Alpoo" proclaimed "leftover dinner for dumb dogs." We were all amazed at this cleverness and suddenly everyone wanted every sticker ever made. I even got Pa to drive me to Telegraph and Nine Mile Road to Hayes Market, another party store outside of most of the Eisenhower kids' realm. They had several "Wacky Packages," which I quickly snapped up.

The craziest "gotta have it" rage was rather short-lived. It featured two glass balls on a string. When you bounced it, they would clack together. This was a load of fun, until someone clacked them together with too much force and the glass shattered. The school principal banned the clacking glass balls.

The principal at Eisenhower had an image problem. He not only banned our favorite fad he could also be downright strange! One time he called the entire student body together and lined us all up on the playground in rows. We stood there while we got a lecture about some wrong deed that someone had done. He wanted to know who did it. I'm sure most of us had no idea what he was talking about, but he thought he was teaching us a lesson. The only lesson I got was that adults could be rather childish at times. First banning clacking glass balls and now this!

THE LITTLE GROWNUP

CHAPTER FIVE
FLYING FEET AND A SQUEEZEBOX

Ma and Pa came to the United States from Germany in the 1950s. They first met each other at one of the German clubs in Detroit. At that time, the German-American population in the Detroit area was large enough to support many social clubs, picnics, German radio shows and even a German newspaper. Ma and Pa attended functions at the Carpathia Club and the Saxon Hall. They involved me in the clubs' youth dance groups to apparently give me some German heritage education.

The "Schuhplattler" is the famous German folk dance from Bavaria. The men wear leather shorts and basically hop around to the music as they slap their breeches to the music. What Bavarian folk dancing has to do with the Germany of my parents, I never did know. Ma was from East Prussia and Pa from the German speaking Siebenbuergen in Romania – neither even close to Bavaria. Somehow the geography didn't matter to the immigrants as they delighted in seeing their offspring dressed in cute little outfits and dancing.

THE LITTLE GROWNUP

I still recall the first practice I attended held in the basement of the instructor's home. Wolfgang Sturm's name even sounded ominous and he looked ancient to me. "Take your hands out of your pockets," he demanded with his thick German accent. I did as I was told. Before the other boys arrived, he was hardly able to demonstrate a few steps before his arthritis kicked in. Soon the other dancers did arrive, but they offered no pep talk or learning tips to the new runt. I was the youngest. They didn't like me.

Luckily these dances didn't require choreography by Fred Astaire and soon I was hopping around and slapping my leather shorts like everybody else. Mr. Sturm actually turned out to be a nice old goat. He was a baker by trade and one Christmas gave us all gingerbread men.

Our group appeared at various German-American events around Detroit always to the accompanying sounds of distorted Oom-pah music compliments of Mr. Sturm's huge reel-to-reel tape player. The highlight of our performances was getting paid by our adoring audience, made up 99.9 percent of our parents and grandparents. We gleefully collected the pennies, dimes, and an occasional quarter they threw at us while we were dancing. Mr. Sturm's arthritis must have taken its toll as later we were in a different group. This time at another club, the Saxon Hall.

More in tune with Pa's heritage, these Saxon folk dances were easier and our outfits classier. Long pants meant my bony knees weren't showing anymore. The arthritic expertise of Mr. Sturm was replaced by the misguided efforts of Kathy Breckner. Mrs. Breckner tried her best, but was totally overwhelmed with a bunch of kids. She

FLYING FEET AND A SQUEEZEBOX

ranted and raved during rehearsals, but that just made us want to ignore her even more. She just didn't understand the priorities her dancers had. It all culminated in one big tantrum when we all abandoned her for the television set in the bar of the Saxon Hall. The viewing event of the century, as far as we were concerned, was taking place! We just couldn't miss the night Fonzie did his big motorcycle jump on the show "Happy Days." Somehow we did learn enough dances to enchant our parents and grandparents as the coins once again flew onto the dance floor during our performances.

Saxon folk dancers Moni and me

One year Mrs. Breckner decided to stage a Christmas concert turning all her little folk dancers into singers. Unfortunately she knew less about music than she did dancing. Her timing on "The Little Drummer Boy" would have had baby Jesu falling out of his manger and mother Mary holding her ears, but the audience endured the slightly mistuned and off beat pa-rum-pa-pa-pumming and parents and grandparents were again beaming with delight, much to the delight of Mrs. Breckner's ego. Actually poor Mrs. B deserved an ego boost after putting up with her crazy group of kids.

Folk dancing in a group apparently wasn't enough for my ego. I also enrolled in tap dance lessons! Perhaps I needed something a bit more American. The Art Linkletter Totten Dance Studio was obviously living in its past glory. Linkletter wasn't even a dancer but a television personality in the 1950s. This dance school seemed to be stuck in that era. Students practiced to and purchased for home use the long outdated 78-rpm phonograph records with such up-to-date 1950s songs as "Tea for Two" or "Satan Takes a Holiday." Of course this was at least twenty years past that time.
   The records featured the voice of a man with a hilarious Brooklyn accent reciting dance steps during the music. "Slap step step. Slap step step. Slap one slap two slap three slap four." Despite my obvious talent I did not become the next miniature Gene Kelly or Art Linkletter for that matter. The dance studio finally made enough money off of my parents, selling pins, trophies and of course those old records and my black tap shoes were retired. The 78-rpm records were enjoyed for many years later as comedy material.

A little aside to my tap dancing lessons is that near the studio was a bagel store, which we would visit. Southfield, Michigan, with its rather large Jewish community, had bagel bakeries in the early 1970s, long before the general population embraced them.

What next after tackling dancing? Maybe it was the German thing to do. Ma played one as a kid. It was played at the German events we attended.

FLYING FEET AND A SQUEEZEBOX

At age eight I started accordion lessons. The heyday of the accordion was in the 1950s. This was the early 1970s. But just like my tap dancing endeavor, I'd rather embrace the past than get caught up in the whim of the day! Every week Mr. Arroll would come to our house for the half-hour private lesson. He drove all over the Detroit area giving these lessons. I wondered why he wasn't on TV instead.

During the week I would practice everything from the "Beer Barrel Polka" to "Battle Hymn of the Republic." The first efforts were on a tiny black learner accordion. Soon I outgrew that and got a beautiful full sized instrument with golden keys and three different treble tone buttons.

The accordion doesn't need any accompaniment as the melody is played with the right hand on a piano-like keyboard while the left hand pushes buttons adding the chordal accompaniment. A perfect solo instrument for a big ham. When guests came over to visit Ma and Pa, they would invariably ask me to play. I'd act all bashful and shy, but soon they had a hard time getting me to shut up.

The accordion might not have been in vogue, but somehow I always ended up playing at the school Christmas program and everyone seemed to enjoy it. Eventually I was even drafted by Mrs. Breckner to accompany the German dance group – no more distorted tape recordings for her now that she found a miniature Myron Floren in her midst!

THE LITTLE GROWNUP

*Borger family
serenaded on a golden accordion*

Bethie Forter was in my class. She lived just down the road from us. She played the piano and since I played the accordion we decided to try to play a duet. I hauled my accordion to her house and we practiced. We weren't savvy enough to realize that even though we both were playing the same song, the music we were using was written in different keys. It sounded more like an orchestra tuning up.

Bethie's mother was from England and seemed like she was always ready for a visit by the Queen for tea. Bethie was put on a pedestal by her parents and she couldn't do anything wrong. I guess they figured out it must be my fault that the duet sounded like it did.

Bethie liked to watch the TV show "The Partridge Family" which was the rage at the time. David Cassidy and Shirley Jones starred in this sitcom about a singing family. The producers struck gold by also releasing many LP albums of music played on the show. I liked the show and the music, too. We would get together and listen to the records.

FLYING FEET AND A SQUEEZEBOX

Our innocent childhood friendship barely withstood the next scandal. I was accused of being in love with Bethie! Unbeknownst to me, some of my schoolmates thought they would play a prank. They cut my picture out of the school yearbook together with Bethie's picture and made a beautiful hand printed card saying how much I loved Bethie. They left it in the Forter mailbox. Her mom found it. She thought it was the sweetest thing she had ever heard of. I'm surprised I wasn't invited over for high tea!

On my next visit I had no idea what she was gushing about until she showed me the card. She wouldn't be convinced that the writing was a fraud and wouldn't even let me clear my name through a handwriting test. Bethie's mom said she would keep the letter in her scrapbook for Bethie to remember her first love letter forever! Bethie didn't seem to come to my defense either. We remained friends, but at school I kept my distance. Having a girlfriend at age nine was simply unacceptable!

Around the time I started taking accordion lessons, my great-grandmother paid us a special visit from Germany. Ma and Pa went on vacation there and brought her back on the airplane with them. She had never flown before and was afraid to fly alone. Before her trip, she sent newspaper articles to Grandma and Ma about planes crashing and people dying. Somehow she overcame her fear and came for a visit. The last time she had visited Detroit was when Ma got married. She took a boat to get to America then. Great-grandmother Hulda lived in the famous Black Forest area of Germany. She had lead a rough life, losing her husband during World War

THE LITTLE GROWNUP

Two, having been forced off of her farm after the war, and eventually relocating to a part of Germany that was new to her.

She enjoyed visiting Grandma and Ma, but I don't think she ever considered moving to the United States. I serenaded her with some of my first accordion songs, but since I didn't speak much German we mostly just hugged and smiled at each other.

CHAPTER SIX
SOAP ON A ROPE AND RICKY RICARDO

Ma and Pa didn't spend any extra money on television sets. I remember the first one we had in Detroit had a tiny black and white picture. TV fascinated me. During the preschool years most of my friends and I were glued to the set for the local kids shows like Bozo (billed as "The World's Most Famous Clown" and we believed it) and later Oopsy the Clown. Locally produced Detroit television was in its heyday when I was growing up. Besides the kiddie's shows, we could also enjoy "Rita Bell's Prize Movie" in the morning. I still recall her catchy theme song "Cotton Candy" by trumpeter Al Hirt.

At 12:30pm it was "The Lucy Show" on Channel 50, "a service of Kaiser Broadcasting". Then the announcer would come on and inform us "It's one o'clock. Time for Detroit's Favorite Movie Host, Bill Kennedy!" The afternoon would progress with an old and most likely boring movie, but Bill Kennedy (or "grumpy man" as we called him) would keep us entertained with his commentary between commercial segments.

THE LITTLE GROWNUP

During school years we missed all of this daytime fun, but after-school programming could keep our attention for hours. By this time we had a "new" used color TV set passed on to us by "Aunt" Marion and "Uncle" Bill who had bought a newer model. The commercials were in color, but many of the shows were still black and white! We watched "The Three Stooges," "Speed Racer," "The Brady Bunch," "The Addams Family," "Hogan's Heroes," and "The Little Rascals." Channel 50 definitely had a lock on the after-school audience. The next day at school these shows would often be the topic of discussion. Channel 50 also provided my first exposure to a show that would become a lifelong addiction.

The 1950s sitcom "I Love Lucy" was my obligatory viewing every weeknight. Lucille Ball and Desi Arnaz became my idols. Although the reruns were still quite popular, no one had tapped into the huge marketing of Lucy products so pervasive today. That didn't frustrate me! I produced my own fan articles. Cutting out a picture of the Arnazes, I sent it to a poster company and had my own poster made for my bedroom. I had a sweatshirt produced with the words "Lucy-Desi Power" emblazoned on it. I was a fan.

Channel 50 was my Lucy station and their studios were just up the road a bit from Grandma and Grandpa's house. I thought it would be a great place to work some day. Broadcasting sounded like the future I had picked for myself. Not only did they show "I Love Lucy" on a regular basis, Desi Arnaz had also made a recent appearance there on the "Lou Gordon Show." Gordon had a sometimes controversial talk show interviewing various local and national celebrities and politicians.

SOAP ON A ROPE AND RICKY RICARDO

I was in heaven when Arnaz came to Detroit to promote his autobiography entitled "A Book." I tried calling into the show when his interview came on, but found out it had been pre-taped. The good news was that he was going to be at Northland Mall to sign his new book. Of course I pestered Ma to no end and she agreed to take me to the book signing. It was a once in a lifetime meeting for me. Mr. Arnaz had accomplished so much during his lifetime, marrying the beautiful Lucy, starring and producing in their landmark series, and owning the famed Desilu Studios.

The man at the mall was still larger than life but a bit saddening. He hadn't aged well and certainly didn't look like Ricky Ricardo anymore. He still did have the same hat Ricky wore. He had a cigar in one hand and a glass of beer close by as he graciously chatted with the fans and signed their books. I asked him if he would ever return to television in a special with Lucy. He said, "I would love to, but it's up to her." He signed my copy of his book "To Hans. Gracias! Desi Arnaz." I also brought along a copy of an "I Love Lucy" biography written by someone else. He hesitated signing it at first, saying it was full of mistakes. He then inscribed it "I forgive the author," and signed his name.

Unfortunately we didn't bring a camera along. I'm sure the picture of me with white haired Desi Arnaz would have become a full sized poster, too! Monika once got to go on the "Bozo the Clown Show" and Kurt got to meet Spiderman at the Tel-Twelve Mall once (a man dressed up in tights jumping up and down on a trampoline). But I got to meet an American television genius!

My sister Monika had a very caring godmother "Aunt" Nancy. Caring that is toward Moni. Unfortunately, my brother Kurt and I got lost in

THE LITTLE GROWNUP

the shuffle. Around Christmas time we would usually visit "Aunt" Nancy, who was one of Ma's best friends from her school days. "Aunt" Nancy relished her role as godmother and showered Moni with gifts including various and sundry Barbie doll accessories. Kurt and I were pretty jealous as we didn't get any gifts at all and felt left out. Somehow Ma hinted at this discrepancy in "Aunt" Nancy's love.

"Please Santa, no soap on a rope!"

The next Christmas came and sure enough Moni got her due again, but there were two extra presents under the tree. One for Kurt and one for me. Gleefully we opened our boxes up. Maybe it was a GI Joe doll or at least a Matchbox car? Not exactly. It was soap on a rope and a pair of socks. Identical packages for both of us. Soap on a rope. Socks. All is calm. All is bright. We smiled the best we could and acted happy. Maybe too happy as the next year Monika once again got a toy she wanted. Once again we got soap on a rope and socks.

SOAP ON A ROPE AND RICKY RICARDO

In fact, for years later soap on a rope and socks became the joke gift we would give each other long after we had outgrown being jealous over "Aunt" Nancy's adoration of Moni. Looking back now I still think very highly of this special "Aunt" as she really was a nice lady! Oddly enough, Moni said that despite her shower of gifts, she was a bit afraid of Nancy. Since she was my sister's godmother, Moni always feared that if something ever happened to our parents, she would have to go live with her. I don't really know why she had this fear. After all, she didn't get the soap on a rope.

While my sister played with her Barbie doll camper and my brother had the companion Ken camper, I never had such a luxury. I had something better. Ma had an almost up-to-date 1960s Frigidaire icebox that had a large metal fold down compartment with plastic top to hold produce and keep it fresh. When the Frigidaire was replaced with a newer model, I asked for this spectacular drawer. My vivid imagination had already invented the "fruit bin camper."

This "fruit bin camper" was part submarine. I took it in the bathtub. It was part modern motor home. It provided a home for GI Joe next to Barbie and Ken's lame plastic camper. All went well until one day GI and his humble abode were invaded by Kurt's foot as he stepped on it while traipsing through the basement. The plastic top broke and the "fruit bin camper" era ended.

Southfield was growing and needed new facilities. I was already treated to the brand new Eisenhower Elementary School and now we had Beechwoods Recreation Center just up the road. Moni loved the indoor skating rink there, but I liked the hot summer days at the new public swimming pool. Ma and all of us had annual passes and just like most kids, I loved the water. Beechwoods pool had the nerve to ban kids for fifteen minutes every hour for an adult swim. That wasn't fair to keep me out of the water while a select few grownups got to enjoy the pool all to themselves! No belly flops, splashing or noise was noticed in the pool during that time. What a bunch of boring swimmers!

Beechwoods also had a brand new library and it became another favorite haunt. I especially liked to check out the old time radio show cassette tapes. It was fun to listen to the stars of the 1940s and 1950s like Jack Benny and Bob Hope. The librarian got to know me quite well. She found out that I played the accordion. She invited me to bring it to the library. That was probably the only time in the history of Southfield Public Library that the customers were serenaded with "Liechtensteiner Polka" while they were trying to find a copy of the latest novel to borrow!

Ma and Pa attended the Emmanuel Lutheran Church in Southfield. The church was located on Lahser road, which Pa and most everyone else pronounced "lasher." At one time Ma taught a Sunday school class there. I went to the classes, too and it was an excellent grounding to my Christian faith. I am glad my parents realized the importance of teaching children about God at an early age. By knowing where I came from, I had the coping mechanisms for later in life. "Jesus Loves Me" is easy to sing as a child but even better to be able to recall in adult difficulties.

My love for music was accented as we sang the old hymns of the church in our little classroom. We even had our own pianist in the Sunday school who pounded on the piano keys very loudly,

SOAP ON A ROPE AND RICKY RICARDO

causing the kids to sing "Praise God From Whom All Blessings Flow" even louder.

Easter was a special time at the church, as the ladies would host a church breakfast featuring Finnish pancakes. Delicious! Of course Christmas was a glorious time and the wonderful Christmas carols echoed through that church sounding like angels were singing. I don't remember much about the actual sermons, except they seemed to go on forever. The wooden pews seemed hard after about ten minutes.

The church put together a pictorial directory one year, and of course the Borgers had to be featured as well. Ma and Pa dressed us all up and took us to the church at the appointed time. We may have been well dressed, but our attention span was limited. The photographer must have used up a roll of film. In one picture Monika is making a face. In another Kurt had his eyes closed. I admit I wasn't too photogenic either with my grimace. Ma and Pa looked composed. I guess they were used to it as our home pictures mirrored the church experience. They finally chose a shot for the directory with their less than perfect child models.

Grandma still kept her membership at Holy Cross Lutheran Church in Detroit. I don't know if it was out of nostalgic reasons or because she couldn't find a Lutheran church she liked in Farmington Hills. The area around Holy Cross in Detroit had deteriorated and she rarely attended there anymore, if at all. Located on Grand River at Whitcomb, the stone edifice of Holy Cross was quite impressive. Grandpa always took her to the church for her annual roast beef dinner pilgrimage, which I was invited to go along for. We would enter the church and wait in the pews before being ushered into the dining hall when our turn came up. Even though most of the parishioners had moved to the suburbs, the church was still quite active and the annual dinner was quite a popular event.

Grandpa regularly attended St. Clare's Catholic Church in Farmington Hills. I often went with him. I admired Grandpa's dedication. Father Drogowski, the priest there, seemed very kind and always had something nice to say to me on the way out. With my Protestant upbringing though, I found the petitions to Mary, the statues, and the rote prayers odd. I liked being there with Grandpa though and felt God was watching over us regardless of which church I was in that week.

CHAPTER SEVEN
WILDWOOD DAYS

One summer I was obsessed with bugs, butterflies and cocoons. I had a special plastic bug collection chamber and my summer prize was a cocoon that a caterpillar spun inside my bug catcher. I was waiting for it to turn into a butterfly. It seemed like it was taking forever as the summer wore on.

Hurray! Grandma and Grandpa invited me to go camping with them. What about my cocoon? It was invited along, too. Grandma and Grandpa didn't camp very often anymore, so I felt very privileged to be in on this adventure. Their huge yellow tent, Coleman stove and sleeping bags hadn't been used in a while. And inside the tent we would get to sleep on the army cots. Sometimes us kids were allowed to sleep on these cots while staying over at Grandma and Grandpa's house – and our imaginations conjured up the soldiers who undoubtedly had slept on these cots

THE LITTLE GROWNUP

through many wars and maybe even died on them.

Anyhow, one of Grandpa's friends opened a private campground called "Rambler's Roost" somewhere in rural Michigan. It promised nature trails, swimming hole and beautiful campsites. Grandpa, Grandma, my cocoon and I were ready to rough it. We expected most everything, except the mosquitoes and black flies that awaited us. We noticed the swarm of bugs when we arrived and quickly sprayed insect repellent on our bodies. We'd be able to brave this out!

The tent was pitched. The bugs must have seen me hanging my bug collector and cocoon on a hanger outside the tent and they were mad. We took a walk down the trail. The bugs swarmed over our heads like dark clouds. They especially seemed attracted to Grandpa's red shirt, which he finally took off and used as a fan to try to keep them from annoying him. This of course only brought them my way or towards Grandma.

We quickly nixed the idea of swimming, as we didn't want to offer a flesh sacrifice to the bugs. Swatting bugs and mosquitoes wasn't much fun. We survived one night at Rambler's Roost before rambling on to the more civil and apparently insect repellant sprayed Bishop Lake State Park.

I remember that the drinking water at Bishop Lake smelled like rotten eggs, but at least the bug problem was gone. Incidentally, weeks later the still unhatched cocoon finally opened to reveal a beautiful monarch butterfly. It never did seem to have suffered at all from its tour of several Michigan campgrounds.

The great outdoors became synonymous with Wolverine, Michigan as several times a year we could head "up north" from the city. We'd pile in the Ford Country Squire station wagon. Before leaving home, Kurt, Moni and I had to fight as to who would get to sit in the back of the station wagon, which had its own little popup seat. With this finally decided, our entourage would head up the highway. Behind the station wagon was our camper home; No more tenting for us! This "Holiday Traveler" 1950s model had plenty of room for a family of five.

The "are we almost there?" mentality lasted most of the six-hour ride up I-75. Finally we'd arrive in Wolverine, Michigan and we knew our destination was getting closer when we passed the old barn that was almost fallen down. When the station wagon turned down Wurm road, we were almost there!

My parents had high hopes for Wolverine. In the early 1970s they bought a lot in Wildwood Valley Estates, a fledgling vacation community with promises of lakes, swimming pools, ski lodge, golf course, and leisure living. The original brochure promised "Michigan's ever burgeoning industrial growth together with its population explosion makes ownership of land for leisure living in beautiful northern Michigan an unusually sound investment...Whether for profit or for family health and happiness, an investment in Wildwood Valley Estates is well worth looking into."

Shortly after their purchase of the lot in Wildwood Valley Estates, my parents found out that the developers went bankrupt. It would be the best thing that could happen for three kids. The ski lodge closed. We had no swimming pool, golf course, or electricity. We had a small piece of property. On a sandy road. No neighbors. No houses. Just wilderness. We were in paradise.

We'd cut ferns to make a carpet in front of our camper. We also cut ferns to cover up our

THE LITTLE GROWNUP

bathroom piles. The toilet in the camper couldn't accommodate all of those deposits, so we used nature. Nighttime meant campfires, roasted marshmallows, and the sound of coyotes howling. They sounded creepy, but snuggled up in a sleeping bag in the camper we felt safe. One night we were wakened by the sound of thieves. Raccoons had gotten into some hamburger buns. Pa ran out of the camper in his underwear and chased the coons up a tree.

Daytime adventures included walking through the woods and seeing if the old abandoned Firebird car was still there. Acres and acres of woods were available for us to explore. Pa had an excellent sense of direction and we would walk for hours. I had no idea how he did it, but we always got back with no problems.

Wild blackberries and raspberries grew abundantly on the side of the roadways and we picked and ate and ate and picked. One time they were so plentiful Ma and Grandma set up a canning factory in the camper and canned jam.

Sometimes we would venture over to Echo Lake, which was a manmade unfinished lake the Wildwood developers had planned. Huge stones were strewn all over and we explored with amazement. Wildwood Lake existed as well. This is where a beach was supposed to have materialized. It was never completed, however we did swim there when the snakes or weeds didn't scare us away.

A day trip might take us to the town of Indian River where we would visit the huge wooden cross, apparently carved out of one huge tree and advertised as the biggest crucifix in the world. Very impressive. Right down the road from there was Burt Lake where we didn't have to worry about the weeds or snakes, but since this was a

WILDWOOD DAYS

state park there were more people than in our Wolverine solitude.

Gaylord wasn't too far either. Our favorite there was the Call of the Wild Museum, which featured real animals stuffed and displayed in natural settings. The deer crossing the road and staring into the headlights of an oncoming car seemed very realistic since we saw many deer in the Wolverine area.

Game Haven was also a tourist trap near Wolverine. Their live animals were an amazing sight to a bunch of city grown kids. Wolverine itself was a village we said you would miss if you blinked. It did feature an old-fashioned barbershop, which Pa would take us to. The party store downtown had a great selection of comic books and I usually picked one from Richie Rich. Sometimes I would be a bit more highbrow and buy a copy of the Northwoods Call newspaper and read about all the happenings in this wonderland.

We usually ate in the camper, but once in while we drove past downtown Wolverine and stopped at the Rainbow Cabins and Restaurant. This unique place had a huge pond stocked with rainbow trout on one side of the restaurant. Diners could fish for their dinner and get a fresh trout. I usually just got a hamburger, but we did get to feed the fish. In the wintertime there was no way our station wagon or camper could make the trip to our Wolverine property, so several times we got to stay at the Rainbow Cabins which were cozy but rustic and reminded me of what it must have been like in the days of Lincoln.

Sometimes Pa would venture a little further north on I-75 and we'd beg him to stop at Sea

THE LITTLE GROWNUP

Shell City. Their billboard advertising campaign up and down the highway made it seem like we'd be missing something on the caliber of Disney World if we didn't stop. This tourist trap did appear to be transported right from Florida directly to sleepy northern Michigan. Thousands of sea shells were there for purchase along with thousands of trinkets none of us needed but we all wanted, whether it be a sea shell coated lamp or a plastic alligator. The actual store never seemed to meet the billboard promises as far as Pa was concerned, but somehow he always stopped.

Although Wolverine was our vacation paradise, our backyard in Southfield wasn't bad either. Pa's five acre piece of property was large enough to leave part of the backyard in its natural state. Ma even had some magnificent wild trilliums and jack-in-the-pulpit flowers growing back there, some of which I think she probably transplanted from the wilds of Wolverine.

Snowy weather made a great wonderland back there and Grandma would pull us around on our sled. One year the entire backyard flooded out and turned into what we dubbed "Flu Lake," so named because it froze providing a great natural skating rink and leading us to get sick spending so much time outside. Over the years, this backyard entertained us with everything from a playhouse to sandbox to portable above ground swimming pool.

The grounds were entirely fenced in, providing running area for our labrador retriever Freckles. Freckles unfortunately met his early demise when he dug himself a hole under the fence and promptly got run over on Nine Mile Road. Then another dog Blackie replaced him.

WILDWOOD DAYS

Going out to eat with a family of three kids didn't happen as often as it does today. Occasionally we would re-unite with "Aunt" Marion and "Uncle" Bill and visit Uncle John's Pancake House somewhere on Woodward in Detroit. This place was marvelous! It had to be when an uncle owned it! You could choose from what seemed like an endless variety of pancake flavors and toppings, even for supper. Even fussy eater Kurt could find something. Pa really liked going out for breakfast or maybe it was just more affordable. Another favorite place was the Grecian Palace on Telegraph and Ten Mile. They had a breakfast special that was only a buck or so and we looked forward to these outings.

When I was with Grandpa, he would take me to Elias Brothers' Big Boy. I felt like a big boy ordering what he ordered. We usually sat at the lunch counter and ordered the "Big Boy" sandwich. Blue cheese dressing was the norm on the salad. We would have a Vernors ginger ale to drink. After all, it was made in Detroit. Once in a while we would vary from the "Big Boy" hamburger and have a "Brawny Lad" sandwich, which was also quite good. That hamburger was on a special dark pumpernickel type bun. When we left, I always took the free Big Boy comic book which was marked "ten cents, but free to our guests." Big Boy had a birthday club and that meant on my birthday I would get a free sandwich. The management knew how to cultivate loyal customers. Unfortunately years later Big Boy got rid of Vernors on their menu. The Elias moniker has been dropped. The Big Boy sandwich doesn't seem as big as it was when I was a boy. I don't think they have the comic books any more. I still go.

THE LITTLE GROWNUP

CHAPTER EIGHT
THE BALLOON ROOM
AND BITTER LEMON

Grandma and Ma decided to go strawberry picking one afternoon. After looking through ads in the paper, they found a place, which was, located an hour's drive away from our home. Finding their buckets, which they were anxious to fill with plump berries, they got into the car and took a leisurely drive out to the farm. Much to their surprise, they found out that the "u pick" farm was only open for a few hours a day, starting at 7 AM. The plantation was closed, so back home they went with the plastic pails empty.

Later that week, they decided to drive out to the farm again. This time I was invited. When we arrived, we were told to only pick in the area "that had the big strawberry on top of the truck." I guess the owners didn't want the whole plantation overrun, so they had set aside a certain area, and designated it as the field open for picking that day. They placed a huge papier-mâché' strawberry on the roof of a truck, so the customers would know where to park and pick. After being handed the

THE LITTLE GROWNUP

quart boxes by the employees, we starting picking the berries.

The dew was still on the ground at this early hour, and already the mosquitoes were awful. I thought to myself that this was really a lot of work for a few measly berries, and it was pretty uncomfortable. Grandma and Ma continued to pick though, so I didn't say anything. My basket of berries wasn't getting very full either. I had been eating more than I was putting in the basket. Mounding the berries into a very large heap in the quart baskets, Grandma finally had had enough and decided she had better go and pay for her portion of the berries. The employees of the farm then told her that she had overloaded her baskets.

A sign, where she paid, said that the berries had to be even with the rims of the containers. The berries in Grandma's baskets were bulging over, so that not one more berry would fit into them. The clerk told her she would have to pay extra. Grandma, telling the people she hadn't seen the sign and didn't know the rule, wheedled her way out of paying for the excess berries. I even think that in later trips to the farm, she always used the same excuse, and she never had to pay for the overfilled boxes.

I don't know how many strawberries were brought home, but for the next week we ended up eating strawberries in every form imaginable. We had strawberry shortcake, strawberries in Jell-O, strawberry tarts, and strawberries and cream. Our kitchen turned into a canning factory. Jams and jellies rolled off the assembly line, as the pile of supplies finally diminished. With all the strawberry dishes, we soon grew tired of them. Next June, Ma asked if we should go picking

THE BALLOON ROOM AND BITTER LEMON

again. I must have forgotten the calamity we had had the year before. I said "yes!"

Michigan's summertime strawberries give way to apples in the fall. A trip to the orchard to pick apples in the cool autumn air was a welcome weekend outing. Picking a crisp apple off of a tree and immediately eating it was a boyhood treat. The Northern Spy apple looked quite ugly, but the name sounded mysterious. They were a bit sour but they were my favorite.

Today a visit to the apple cider mill is a visit to a tourist trap. It wasn't quite as commercial when I was growing up. There were already a few cider mills back then that featured the greasy doughnuts and expensive cider. That was ok in a pinch, but not for an experience with Grandpa. One year Grandpa loaded us in the car and told us he was taking us to the "real" cider mill. Somewhere in Romeo, Michigan he finally told us we had arrived.

We all thought he was crazy, as he had driven up to someone's house. No sign of a cider mill evident. He then proceeded to knock on someone's front door. Sure enough, the guy had a cider mill in his barn out back. We saw and experienced true apple cider being pressed. Of course we bought a gallon or two to take home with us and didn't drink it fast enough before it tasted like vinegar. No preservatives in that cider!

Grandma and Grandpa's house on Castlereigh in Farmington Hills became the home that I still idealize today. I'm sure a lot of it has to do with the many memories that were made there, but the place itself typified the American dream home of the 1970s. A sprawling ranch style, it not only had a huge living room but also a front room. Off of the kitchen was a large dining area, but it also boasted another formal dining room adjacent to the front room.

Grandma worked at J.L. Hudson's department store for years and she used her money to help furnish the home with exquisite taste. The kings in their castles couldn't have had it nicer. The front room had a beautiful gold fabric couch. Over it hung a wonderful large painting of Alpine mountains. On the far end of the room were two comfortable upholstered chairs, one for Grandpa and one for Grandma. Grandpa would sit in his chair for hours perusing his Detroit Free Press or Croatian newspaper, the Zajednicar. The light to read by was provided by a magnificent Italian table lamp with marble base, gold ornate bottom globe and two cherub angels peaking out from under the lampshade.

Next to Grandma's chair was a wooden cabinet containing a treasure trove of records, everything from Grandpa's old 78s from the big band era to Grandma's German Christmas LPs. The adjacent dining room had a grandmother clock in it, which marked the top of every hour with Westminster chimes, along with an abbreviated version every 15 minutes.

The living room had dark red shag carpeting, a fireplace, and enough shelving to hold Grandpa's extensive elephant collection along with his golfing trophies. Sometimes I'd look at the various trophies and was quite proud that my Grandpa had won "Third Place Ford Tool and Die 1948 Tournament." Grandpa would spend hours watching all the golf tournaments on TV and he analyzed the players' technique to try and improve his own swing.

As mentioned, the living room also housed his elephant figurine collection, which featured pachyderms in all different colors and sizes. Some must have been worth quite a bit but my favorite was the little gray plastic elephant whose feet would walk when Grandpa put it on an incline. By keeping us entertained with this inexpensive toy, he knew we wouldn't bother his other prizes.

The upstairs had three bedrooms, one for Baba, one for Grandma and Grandpa, and one for guests. The guest room had Grandma's sewing basket and sewing machine in it. Grandma and Grandpa's bedroom had a wall unit air conditioner in it, something quite novel and extravagant for that time. Summers in Michigan can get quite humid and when that happened, Grandma and Grandpa would sleep well while the rest of the house roasted in the humidity. The house was heated in winter by a steam heating system through long heating registers along the walls. If I close my eyes I can sometimes almost hear the clicking of those heating registers as I picture myself in that house.

The kitchen on Castlereigh had a faucet with the best tasting tap water the city of Farmington Hills provided and the best I'd ever tasted. I don't actually know if it was the water or the Ford Motor Company Tool and Die logo drinking glasses that made the water so tasty. Grandma paid her dues with her closet sized kitchen in Detroit. Now she had a modern stove with oven built into the wall. No more oven pilot light problems. It was electric.

Grandma whipped up lots of memorable meals. She still grated potatoes by hand to make potato pancakes; her onion rings were the best. Grandpa loved his sweets and Grandma complied with everything from homemade oatmeal cookies (my favorite) to pumpkin pie with freshly whipped cream. Grandpa worked odd shifts at Ford's in Dearborn and she always packed his metal lunchbox with homemade sandwiches and goodies.

I recall staying with them once when he returned home quite late from work. I was told we would have a treat when he came home but would have to take a nap first. When Grandma woke me up she had made a homemade pizza, which we greeted Grandpa with when he came through the door. This was long before take out pizza parlors were on every corner.

My brother, sister and I always seemed to have more leeway to play at Grandma's place. Oma was always worried we would break something or get something dirty. Her house was immaculate and she also had some beautiful paintings on her walls, including one of deer running through the woods. She had an old windup mantel clock from Germany, which like Grandma's clock would chime several times an hour. She also had a cuckoo clock. If we begged her long enough she would turn the clock hands ahead so we wouldn't have to wait to see and hear the cuckoo.

Oma had a couple of black leather swivel chairs in her living room, perfect for three grandchildren to turn into revolving amusement park rides like we had ridden on our trips with Aunt Dorothy to Cedar Pointe in Ohio. Apparently these chairs had steel balls inside them making them able to revolve. Oma would have a heart attack when we'd whirl the chairs around. "The balls will break and then the chairs won't turn anymore! Stop it!" she would inevitably say during every visit. We'd inevitably try to get away with it every time.

Oma could also be a bit of a fusspot as far as keeping her house clean. In fact she often told the story about how she vacuumed every day. One time she told Opa that he could help around the house a bit, too and volunteered him to do some of the vacuuming in the living room while she was in the back of the house doing some cleaning. Soon she happily heard the vacuum running, but she then noticed it didn't sound quite right. She returned to the living room to find the vacuum turned on but not being used while Opa read the paper. When quizzed about what he was doing, he replied, "As long as you hear the vacuum running you are happy!" Needless to say she wasn't.

Because of Oma's cleaning frenzy she would usually have a conniption fit if we touched her piano. Somehow we always did "play" it and she always complained about us getting our fingerprints all over it. Aunt Dorothy had taken piano lessons years ago, but hadn't tickled the ivories in a long time. The piano was out of tune but since I played the accordion I could get a few songs out of it. Oma never was too amused by it all, but since I was her godson, she was a bit more lenient with me.

One year Aunt Dorothy secretly tape-recorded an hour or so of a Christmas Day when we were there. Listening to that recording years later I'm surprised the adults didn't all end up crazier than a bedbug. Kurt got a toy machine gun that year. Actually anyone who bought him a gift like that deserved the consequences. The hour long tape has him constantly shooting the thing off with its loud "rat-at-tat-at-tat" clacking in the background as Grandma, Grandpa, Ma, Pa, Oma and Opa carry on the semblance of a conversation.

THE LITTLE GROWNUP

Kurt shows off his Christmas gun

Usually Monika, Kurt and I would eventually retreat to Oma and Opa's basement, where out of Oma's sight she couldn't worry as much about our fingerprints ruining her furniture. Aunt Dorothy had a huge bookshelf running the entire wall of the basement and she had a very nice collection including some early Peanuts comic books written in German. We couldn't really understand the German, but it was interesting to see that Charlie Brown and Snoopy looked almost like their American counterparts, albeit a bit younger!

On the other side of the basement was a bar, which was more for decoration than anything else. Oma had a spare refrigerator in there but I don't even recall any liquor being stocked. We amused ourselves playing bartender and customer and serving each other bottles of pop.

Sometimes we'd venture into Opa's workshop. Opa had a workshop in the basement where he spent a lot of time tinkering on various projects. It smelled like wood, glue, paint, and cigars. Opa was an excellent carpenter and built many things

THE BALLOON ROOM AND BITTER LEMON

from scratch. More amazing to me was that he could take an old television or radio shell someone threw away and turn it into a wonderful cabinet. Opa smoked King Edward cigars, which don't exactly have the greatest aroma to them. Oma of course admonished him to only smoke outside. Since his basement workshop was his domain, he would sneak a smoke once in a while, only to be found out by Oma as the cigar smell wafted upstairs through the heating vents. Oma says he also had a "secret" stash of alcohol down in the workshop which he would take a nip of now and then. She knew exactly where it was.

Opa relaxing

Oma and Opa's home on Saratoga had a special guest bedroom dubbed "The Balloon Room," so named because the ceiling had balloon themed wallpaper on it. Before going to bed in The Balloon Room, Oma always made sure I brushed my teeth. One night I accidentally saw her taking her dentures out and she told me, "You can do that with your teeth, too. Just pull on them." I couldn't figure out what I was doing wrong.

It was a great honor for me to be invited to stay over in The Balloon Room, but it was even better when I got to sleep on the couch in Oma and Opa's bedroom. Looking back I'm not quite sure why this was more fun than The Balloon Room, since Opa snored quite loudly and would keep me awake.

Meals prepared by Oma were feasts, whether it was a breakfast consisting of raisin and apple pancakes with Russian breakfast tea or a Thanksgiving Day turkey with all the trimmings. All except one trimming, that is. We always had a good laugh after almost every holiday meal there, since as complete as Oma was in her preparation, she always forgot to put her Jell-O salad on the table. Invariably the meal would be over and she would say, "Oh no, I forgot to put out the Jell-O again!"

Oma and Opa had led an interesting life and once in a while we'd get a glimpse into their past. Opa was born in a German area of Romania and after World War Two he ended up in Germany where he met Oma. Apparently the United States sounded pretty good to many Europeans who had lost everything during the war. Opa was sponsored by a church organization and ended up in North Dakota. He was treated more like an indentured servant than a welcome immigrant and didn't take to his new lifestyle at all. Eventually some distant American relatives helped him get to Ohio and he eventually settled in Michigan.

THE BALLOON ROOM AND BITTER LEMON

True love lured Oma to America to visit Opa. She always said she had enough money to get back to Germany if she wanted to, but she stayed. Her stories of the early years in the United States would be retold and retold. She and Opa washed outside windows for a dollar and the people were so mean they wouldn't even offer them a drink of water. She told about how they started out with practically nothing and how they scrimped and saved for everything. She had her expensive German china dishes and silverware with her to sell if things would get too bad.

Pa was still stuck in Romania at this time. His real mother had died and now his new stepmother and Opa, a.k.a. his father, wanted him to be able to come to the United States as well. Their efforts were long and hard, as Romania was a communist country and no one could leave. The Romanian government had some loopholes for those who paid enough money. Somehow Oma and Opa accomplished all of this and that is how Pa came to the United States. Pa also had a sister in Romania. Oma and Opa later arranged for her to come to the United States for a visit. For some reason she didn't stay, and returned to communist Romania for a rather dreary future.

Oma, Aunt Dorothy, Pa and Opa around the time Pa arrived in the USA

THE LITTLE GROWNUP

One summer Oma, Opa and Aunt Dorothy took me along on a vacation to visit some relatives near Buffalo, New York. I stayed in The Balloon Room the night before the trip, as we intended to leave early the next morning. Despite getting up at dawn, it was several hours past then when we actually left. Oma had to provide us with a full course breakfast, then of course do all the dishes. She then proceeded to vacuum. Then she made the beds. Then she did some more cleaning. Opa of course couldn't get her to leave the house before it was ready for a Spic N Span commercial. "If anything happens to us on the trip, I don't want anyone to find my house a mess," was Oma's comment.

Oma had also volunteered to do some of the driving. By this time Oma and Opa had a very nice Mercury. Oma had previously driven her white Ford Comet for years. Like so many cars of the era, the Comet was quite stylistic. The back taillights looked like two bright red slanted alien eyes! The Comet was the appropriate name for Oma's car, as she had quite a lead foot and drove about as fast as a comet.

Our trip to the Buffalo area would take us through Canada. I'm not sure if the Canadian speed limit was higher than Michigan's or if Oma thought she was on the German autobahn. Part of the trip was on a road with only one lane going either direction. Oma was getting quite frustrated tailgating the driver ahead of her. Aunt Dorothy finally gave her instructions. "Flash your headlights a couple of times so the driver knows you are going to pass, and then step on the gas and pass!" Oma a.k.a "Leadfoot Hildegard" did so and quickly zoomed passed the slowpoke, much to

THE BALLOON ROOM AND BITTER LEMON

my delight and probably giving Opa a heart attack. The trip to Buffalo had probably never been accomplished in that short of a time.

I enjoyed being the center of attention, as Monika and Kurt weren't invited on this trip. The people we stayed with, Gottlieb and Annie Zeintl, had a large farm complete with an above ground swimming pool which was quite a treat to enjoy all by myself. Opa helped the Zeintls with their bee apiary there and he harvested honey, the darkest and best tasting honey I've ever eaten. Evenings were usually spent by the grownups chatting and having a drink or two. Their soda pop selection left a lot to be desired so I was stuck drinking something called bitter lemon, which apparently was used in mixed drinks. After several days I got used to it. Dorothy and I got a bit bored, so we volunteered to put on a German dance exhibition in their living room, which Gottlieb filmed on his home movie camera for posterity.

THE LITTLE GROWNUP

CHAPTER NINE
LIGHTNING BOLT AND THUNDER CLOUD

Pa always claims he worked long hours while we were growing up. I'm sure he did, although he always seemed to have time for us. I don't recall much of what his job as model maker was all about. I know we did visit him once at Delta Model Company and he bought me a Frosty root beer in a bottle out of a vending machine. I wished we had a machine like that at our house.

Pa and I joined the YMCA Indian Guides after I brought home a pamphlet from school. The Indian Guides was a club for fathers and sons only. No women. We would have evening meetings at the YMCA or at other member's homes. With the fascination for all things Indian, boys could live out our fantasies of becoming a pseudo Indian. Every boy and dad had an Indian moniker. I was "Lightning Bolt" and Pa was "Thunder Cloud". We had Indian headbands with feathers and we wore Indian Guide vests covered with various patches especially awarded after participating in different events.

THE LITTLE GROWNUP

Lightning Bolt, Chief Thunder Cloud and North Wind

Events were plenty. During craft time we built balsam airplanes, stilts, leather change purses and snow snakes. We went kiting. We got lost but had a lot of fun driving around Detroit in a scavenger hunt/road rally. One meeting had me talking about the history of music, complete with accordion accompaniment.

Once in a while the YMCA would have us in for an all night lockout. After hours the Indian Guide boys and their fathers took over the whole building. We could use the huge Olympic sized indoor pool, shoot baskets in the gym or do arts and crafts. We could do this all, if we could stay awake. The all night activities usually ended with us filled with pizza and junk food and sleeping in our sleeping bags on exercise mats on the gym floor.

The highlight of the Indian Guide year was when we got to go to Camp Storer or Camp Ohiyesa. Camp Ohiyesa was just a short drive from home in northwest Oakland County, near Highland, Michigan. Ohiyesa seemed like another world.

LIGHTNING BOLT AND THUNDER CLOUD

Located on Fish Lake, it had 300 acres to explore. Camp Storer was a bit further out, in the Irish Hills near Jackson. Both of these YMCA camps had cabins to stay in, a cafeteria with the weakest hot chocolate I've ever tasted, and the best facilities for building a father and son bond.

Depending on the season we could swim in the lake, go horseback riding, toboggan down a huge toboggan slide, or sing around a campfire. Usually a Laurel and Hardy movie would round out the evenings. Kurt joined us for the Indian Guides when he was older and eventually we moved on to the YMCA Trail Blazers, which was for older kids.

Years later Moni admitted she was very jealous of us getting to spend this time with Pa. She was in the Brownies program, but it wasn't the same for her. From what I understand the YMCA Indian Guide program is still around but now does allow daughters. I can't imagine that.

Monika, Ma and Aunt Dorothy were all able to experience life at Camp Storer one summer when we all attended family camp. We all stayed in the same cabin and enjoyed the camp activities, which were set up for family participation. One evening every family was invited to participate in a talent show. Camp Storer has probably never seen the likes of Pa, Ma, Moni, Kurt, Aunt Dorothy and me as we did our rendition of a German folksong about gypsies. This of course was perfect for a show done outside around a blazing campfire. I think even Pa sang in public, which was a once in a lifetime performance for the families camping.

THE LITTLE GROWNUP

proudly wearing our Camp Storer t-shirts at family camp

I loved the YMCA camps so much that I got to attend a whole summer camp week by myself. I did it all. Horseback riding, archery, crafts. The camp staff let us have fun but pushed us to excel. We swam the entire way across the lake just to prove we could do it. Meeting other boys from all over the area, we exchanged addresses so we could stay in touch and we vowed we'd become life long friends. We didn't. The camp created many fond memories though. Camp Storer is apparently still around and still offers those camps. Back then we only escaped watching TV daily, but today's kids can also escape the world of cell phones and computers. What an idea for a vacation!

Between his long work hours and doing activities with us, Pa kept pretty busy. Several times a year he would take Ma out for an evening on the town – most often a dance or dinner at one of the German clubs. When we were too young, they arranged for a local neighborhood girl as a baby sitter to be with us. These sitters usually were eager to play board games with us or amuse us with coloring books and having a little art contest between us.

When we felt we had outgrown the sitters, we protested and got to stay by ourselves. We soon wondered if this was such a good idea. The first time we were alone we all became quite paranoid and were sure someone would break into the house at any moment to kidnap us or kill us. Our imaginations ran wild. The weather that night was oddly windy and the front door actually howled. We decided to stay up and watch late night TV. No way would we be able to go to sleep. An old Sherlock Holmes movie was on. The black and white film captured our attention, as in the dark night of London a murder was committed.
Suddenly real life became just as suspenseful as a wind gust blasted loudly and our front door actually blew open! We were sure the murderer was just about to come through our doorway with a big gun. He didn't however, and after a close inspection of the front porch, our bleary eyes went back to Sherlock. Oddly enough one evening Ma and Pa were driving home from an evening on the town when they heard a shot ring out. One of their car windows was hit and shattered. They never did find out what had happened.

Pa didn't do too much with his buddies, however on rare occasions he went hunting and fishing. His big trophy was a black bear, which he shot during a hunting trip in Michigan's Upper Peninsula. This bear was sent to a taxidermist and mounted as a rug, which was proudly displayed on our front room floor. I was fascinated by this creature, as were Kurt and Moni. We stared at the glass eyes as the bear stared back at us. We wondered if the ferocious looking teeth were real or if they were fake like the big plastic tongue. We took the plastic tongue out of the bear's mouth and examined it. "What are you kids doing? Put that tongue back! How would you like it if I took your tongue out?" Pa caught us and wasn't amused. We would wait until he wasn't around to take a closer look at this plastic artwork again and again.

The bear had a felt backing and over time the hair started to shed. After several years of being on display, having multiple tongue examinations, and shedding more hair than our dog Blackie, Ma finally decided the trophy would be retired to the George Borger hunting museum – better known as the closet. Pa tried to interest me in hunting but I had no interest in killing animals. I was more interested in my live animals, like gerbils and guinea pig. Pa obviously had a gun and I got one, too. My BB Gun provided several hours of fun shooting at targets but it didn't hold my attention very long.

Pa took us all on his small wooden boat to teach us about another sport, fishing. All five of us loaded up early in the morning to get to Bishop Lake State Park in Brighton at sunrise. We had fishing poles, worms, and of course plenty of snacks. We were ready for the excitement of fishing. Our fishing poles were longer than our attention spans. Soon we were bored. We wanted to go swimming! Three splashing children tied to ropes attached to the boat promptly scared away every fish in Bishop Lake, ending the fishing expedition. Bishop Lake State Park was often the destination of family picnics and summer swimming days as well. Other times we would visit the closer Kensington Park.

I learned early that if I wanted something and Ma and Pa wouldn't buy it for me, I could buy it

LIGHTNING BOLT AND THUNDER CLOUD

myself with my own money. I became a newspaper boy for the Southfield Observer newspaper. This local rag consisted of a lot of ads and enough neighborly news to compete with the big Detroit papers. For each paper delivered I got several cents and also a cut from the collections received. I felt very much an adult when I signed my contract as an independent carrier.

The publisher of the paper welcomed me in a special booklet I received. To quote from that letter which I still have: "The training that you receive as an Observer carrier will help you develop character and good habits that will prove valuable to you in later life. It is no accident that over half of the men who today hold public office, boast of the fact that they once carried newspapers."

Unfortunately the publisher didn't tell us about the attack dogs and crabby public. I rode my bicycle up and down McAllister and Hickory Hill with my newspaper bag around my neck filled with the latest edition. Being a paperboy really was a great way of learning the business world. It was a microcosm of society, with both friendly and difficult customers along the route.

The paper was rather unique in that everyone on the block was supposed to get a copy, whether they paid for it or not. This made for rather awkward times when I'd approach a customer's door once a month to try to get some money. "Collecting for the Observer newspaper," I would say as rehearsed. "I never ordered that! Get out of here and don't leave me any more copies!" "But Ma'am...." Door slam. I didn't need this stress in my early youth, so I quickly learned who really didn't want this paper, whether the Observer office thought so or not. I also soon learned which houses to avoid due to vicious dogs that more than once tried to attack their poor paperboy. If I

THE LITTLE GROWNUP

found several issues on the front porch, I assumed they weren't interested, so these folks would be struck from the delivery list, too. The undeliverable extras would be donated to the Indian Guides newspaper drive fundraiser.

The publishers knew it wasn't easy for their delivery boys. Every month the paper would offer a certain premium for getting collections from a certain percentage of the customer route. One month I got a nice dictionary. Another time an umbrella. The highlight of the year was when the premium was a trip with the family to Edgewater Park.

Edgewater was a rather rundown amusement park at Grand River and Seven Mile Road in Detroit. It had seen better days, but to us kids it was almost better than going to the Indian Guides. The newspaper rented the park for an entire evening and we could enjoy all the rides for free. The roller coaster looked like it was from the turn of the century and hadn't been updated since then. The cotton candy they sold was probably just as old. The house of mirrors looked like it was going to fall apart any minute. We loved it. This event was for family members only, but I always brought along some extra "brothers" as my friends jumped at the chance to come along.

One month the Observer was so proud of my accomplishments, they invited me to their office to be interviewed and get my picture taken. I was to be featured as their "Newspaper Carrier of the Month." As I walked in the Observer office door I was given a brand new cloth bag with the company logo on it. I had been using an old worn carrier bag I was given when I started. This wouldn't do for such an important boy. Wow! A new bag! The Observer had merged with the

Eccentric and was now known as the Observer & Eccentric. How's that for a mouthful? I happily beamed for the photographer with the logo emblazoned bag. As soon as the picture was snapped, they took their bag back and congratulated me.

When my article came out, my fame didn't last long. They misspelled my name and most of the story was about how other boys could be a newspaper carrier, too so they could enjoy the great benefits the company offered. "Our carrier is a student away from his classroom. As a carrier for the Observer & Eccentric, Hans is learning basic business skills and attitudes that will be helpful in dealing with people." Traipsing through the cold snowy winters, wasting nice summer vacation afternoons delivering papers, avoiding dogs, and putting up with crabby customers finally took its toll. I had learned the attitudes that were helpful in dealing with people. I quit.

Being a newspaper boy at an elementary school age was the norm for the early 1970s. I doubt that today it would be too safe. The young person's world was a lot more innocent back then and parents weren't worried about letting their kids run loose in the neighborhood. We had bicycles. No one wore a helmet. No one thought of wearing a helmet. No one ever got hurt. We rode our bikes to school unaccompanied when we didn't want to take the school bus.

After school or on weekends we explored the area unaccompanied by adults. We would take our bikes or walk to Nine Mile Road and Beech Daly where we might buy a doughnut at the Southfield Bakery or get frozen custard at "Custard's Last Stand." The plaza also had a party store where we would look over the candy rack, but for some

THE LITTLE GROWNUP

reason the staff there wasn't too friendly toward young customers like us. The oddest store was an Oriental type market and we enjoyed looking at the seaweed food items and strange looking writing on the cans. The place had the oddest odor. Dried fish has a way of smelling a bit. The only thing we bought there was a pair of chopsticks since everything else was a bit weird to us.

One of the first things I bought with my newspaper earnings was a cassette tape recorder. I had been fascinated with the ability to record music and voice onto a machine since watching Pa and his reel-to-reel monstrosity. He took me to Radio Shack and I picked out a machine for $29.95 plus tax. I got my money's worth out of this and soon also bought a small black and white television set. In those days before videotape recorders and DVD players, I recorded "I Love Lucy" audio off of Channel 50. I recorded Mr. Sturm's German music from his huge reel-to-reel machine. The cassette tape recorder became a passion.

Moni and I recorded several ad lib dramas using our imagination to create the script as the plot progressed. These taped shows came complete with musical scores, compliments of the record player blaring in the background. Some of the stories we came up with could rival Hollywood, featuring exotic locations and characters such as talking rabbits! Moni also did a series of documentary shows, reading a book about horses. In between the chapters, I played an interlude on the accordion. I took the tape recorder to school and during recess gathered several friends together at the corner of the playground. We'd experiment with different voices. Elementary school age kids playing with a tape recorder must have looked too ominous. Since we weren't using a swing set or playing tetherball, the teacher got suspicious of potential troublemakers. It was all quite innocent, but my tape recording and I were branded and the tape recorder had to stay at home.

By this time I had built up a small posse of friends who were also interested in tape recorders and the media in general. Since David, Bill, Debbie and I couldn't do tape recording at school, we devised other clandestine operations, including writing and editing newspapers to each other during class! These handwritten issues featured our imaginations running wild. Complete with everything from headlines to "Dear Abby" type help columns to comics, our creativity was at a high. Too bad the teachers couldn't enjoy it!

Later we advanced to producing comic books with color drawings starring superhero versions of ourselves. The old 1960s television program "Family Affair," which was being rerun ad nauseum by then, also became fodder for our comic books with innocent children on that show becoming much more evil and conniving.

The pinnacle of all of this mass media production was a series of recorded "radio shows" we recorded on cassettes at our various homes. Sometimes we would all get together and brainstorm on skits. The shows had recurring characters and themes and are quite amazing to listen to even today. Debbie became one of my best friends and we exchanged tapes for years, amusingly documenting everything from our first jobs to Southfield teachers on strike. I was convinced that broadcasting would be my life and thoroughly enjoyed the microphone and its creative outlet.

THE LITTLE GROWNUP

CHAPTER TEN
TRAINS, PLANES AND A CELLO

We knew almost all of our neighbors in Southfield. Pa was quite social, so I don't know whether it was his friendliness or if neighbors were just more neighborly in my youth than they are now. Our next-door neighbor was an Avon lady. She was very helpful when it came time to buy Ma a birthday or Christmas present. The neighbors on the opposite side of the Avon lady were Mr. and Mrs. Moore. The Moores were Mormons. I don't think we knew any other Mormons. Pa invited them over once to explain their beliefs and they showed us a narrated slide show. Pa liked to hear about different religions, but never seem to pin himself down to any.

Toby and Dorothy Blan lived next to the Moores. Dorothy was a chain smoker, but her real addiction was crossword puzzles. Dorothy had an excellent command of the English language and helped me with English class homework. Oddly enough, Toby and Dorothy were from Tennessee or Kentucky and spoke English like hillbillies. Toby liked to go fishing with Pa and both Toby and Dorothy camped out with us in Wolverine several times.

THE LITTLE GROWNUP

With a masculine name like Toby, he seemed like a tough John Wayne type. Once in Wolverine though he exposed his weakness. A harmless snake slithered out of a log on one of our walks. Toby screamed and jumped so high he looked like a cartoon kangaroo. I always thought Toby's name was cool, unlike my name "Hans." Years later I found out Toby wasn't his real name. It was Herman!

Another neighbor down the road was Dick Rossiter and his wife Dorothy. Dick had retired from the Santa Fe Railroad. That sounded very exotic to me. Dick rolled his own cigarettes using loose tobacco and rolling papers. I didn't appreciate his smoking but watching him make his own cigarettes was pretty cool. I liked hanging out at the Rossiters and once decided it would be more fun to help them rake their fall leaves than help Pa at home. Dick seemed to appreciate it. Pa didn't. The next time I raked at home, even though Pa didn't roll his own cigarettes or have stories about railroad days.

I collected stamps and had a quite a collection thanks to family and friends saving them for me, but eventually stamps were too one-dimensional. I wanted a pet. Not a simple pet. I wanted a special one. During a school field trip to a book fair, I bought a paperback by Sterling North entitled "Rascal." This delightful story of a boy and his pet raccoon got me thinking. I needed a raccoon, too! I became obsessed with getting my own rascal.

It probably wasn't even legal to sell raccoons as pets but somehow by combing through the phonebook I found a place that sold wild animals. Ma and Pa didn't exactly encourage this new passion. They knew that raccoons weren't exactly tamable or happy in a cage. Perhaps they remembered the pet monkey their earlier neighbors had. I started saving my money to buy my new pet.

To speed things up, after all a purchased raccoon was quite expensive, I also got the idea of buying a live animal trap. Perhaps I could catch my own raccoon? After all, they were around even if not physically seen. The evidence of their visits would be obvious the next day as the raccoons' nocturnal visits to find food left a mess of strewn trash from overturned garbage cans.

I sent away for information from the Mustang Trap Company. Soon I had their brochure and a very captivating 45-rpm plastic record, which I played over and over on my record player. A grandfatherly man explained how wonderful and fun Mustang Traps were. I had to have one. The day came when my paper route money was enough to place the order. When it arrived we anxiously set up the trap. For some reason the man on the record had a lot more fun than I did. Except for a couple of squirrels, the raccoons and the rest of the Southfield wildlife avoided my Mustang Trap. When I figured I finally had enough money to buy my pet raccoon, I was easily persuaded to buy an aquarium instead.

Dave's Aquarium Shop, a new pet fish store, opened up around the corner. A corner of the front room became my new undersea world. A ten-gallon aquarium was just big enough to accommodate various types of fish. Since the store was close by, I often would come home with new inhabitants for my tank. One day Dave had something new! What boy wouldn't love an underwater frog in his aquarium? Froggie was very cool looking and I was sure the fish in the tank would love their new friend. He got accommodated to his new surroundings as I watched him swim around. When I came back a while later, I couldn't find one of the neon fish. Soon another one was missing. Froggie was returned to Dave and somehow his belly looked a little fuller than when he arrived. I should have named him Rascal.

Around the time of Dave's Aquarium Shop, a hobby store moved into the same shopping complex. My next short-lived passion became model railroads. Pa took a large board, nailed my HO tracks onto it, and I was in business. Actually the hobby shop got my business. I bought railroad cars, little trees, buildings, signs and artificial grass. One of the cars was marked "Santa Fe" which our already mentioned neighbor and retired Santa Fe employee Dick Rossiter appreciated.

I enjoyed my railroad, but my attention span soon wandered as it wasn't much fun to watch the train go round and around the same track. The cost of supporting the hobby shop was getting to be a bit much for the thrill provided. Instead of buying even more tracks, trees, buildings, signs and artificial grass, it was cheaper to let the train sit in the basement corner forgotten and forlorn.

From trains it was time to move to planes. My school friend Bill and his brother were members of the Civil Air Patrol. They got to wear army-like fatigues and fly in a plane. Bill's brother was quitting the group, so Bill had little difficulty talking me into buying his brother's uniforms at a discount and joining him. At first the Civil Air Patrol sounded interesting and fun. During World War Two its members were called to be on the lookout for enemy planes. I'm not quite sure what the group's task was in the 1970s however. The enemy obviously wasn't flying low through Southfield, Michigan.

The group held meetings, which were quite dull. I hung on as they promised a plane ride and weekend camp. We got the plane ride and the camp was the weekend from hell. Dressed in our uniforms, we became fodder for grownups who were acting like frustrated generals barking orders at us mini soldiers. If I wanted someone barking orders at me, I could have stayed home and listened to Pa. At least he was family! They made us march. They made us salute. I felt like I had been drafted or put in reform school. I wasn't amused by any of it. That was the end of the Civil Air Patrol and me. I quit. Bill quit. I wondered why he was a member in the first place.

Forget airplanes. I decided to stick with my music. If you think the accordion was enough, next I got the great idea to take cello lessons at school! With my love for my Grandpa's big band records and my hot air, the obvious choice would have been the trumpet. But no, one of my friends, David, played the cello. I would be a cellist, too. By signing up, we could be in the same class. Ma and Pa didn't even have to shell out any money for the instrument either as the school had a loaner program. The cello I got was a bit beaten up, but my playing never did merit much else.

The teacher, Mr. Woodson, was obviously into classical music. The music selections, or "pieces" as Mr. Woodson preferred to call them, weren't much fun. Some were downright sleepy with titles like "Sarabande." Unlike the accordion there was no "Too Fat Polka" or "Love Me Tender" on this practice schedule. Our class met in the home economics class kitchen. A picture of me playing the cello next to a stove provided enough of a contrasting image to make it in the school yearbook.

playing a "piece" in the home-ec room

Ma and Pa never really encouraged the cello, but they didn't discourage it either. Mainly they gritted their teeth at this latest musical adventure. My bow glided over the strings with the less than melodious practicing. I wanted to be as good as David but never could get his technique. We must have been okay as we attended a few school competitions. Mr. Woodson did his best.

Suddenly Moni decided she wanted to play the violin. I'm not sure if the reason for her decision was having a friend in the class. This time Ma and Pa didn't get off as cheap as they had to buy her a violin. Now they had high pitched screeching to listen to along with the moaning groaning sounds of my cello. Kurt must have felt left out. So he thought up the idea of guitar lessons. After one lesson he decided it was too much work and opted for a much more successful after school baseball career. Moni and I developed our string instrument finesse for a couple of years before retiring our rosin and our bows.

During my youth we never dreamt of digital cameras or video recordings to preserve memories. The preferred method of the day was the slide show. Whether it was Grandpa, Opa, or Pa, they all took slides and they all would present their camera work at our various gatherings. This was not as simple as it may sound. First they had to drag out the equipment. This consisted of a bulky slide projector and a large screen, which magically appeared when pulled out of a metal tripod casing. For the slideshow they had an ever growing and seemingly endless supply of either round carousels that fit the projector or in the case of Grandpa's machine, a plastic tray that was placed in it.
The technology was rather primitive compared to today's computer generated images, but it provided beautiful sharp images of whatever the photographer snapped. Grandpa was the most prolific photographer as it was his hobby. His Kodacolor slides preserved that era so crisply that the images look like they will almost speak.
Grandpa's slide projector didn't hold as many pictures as Pa's machine, so the show would be interrupted every thirty-six pictures so he could change the slide tray. His machine didn't even have an automatic changer so after every slide, you heard him advance the projector manually. Clunk, clunk! It did have a rather nice metal pointer built in to it that Grandpa would invariably use to point out various features we might have missed. "This picture was taken of your mother when she was a cheerleader at school," he said as he took the pointer and

indicated where young Irene was in case we didn't recognize her.

The slide trays all fit into several wooden boxes especially made for them. For some reason despite all of this organization, every time we saw the slides, some would be mixed up. "There is Martha and me in Germany," Grandpa said. Then the next slide he would proclaim, "Oh, now this was at the New York World's Fair." And the next picture would be in their living room Christmas 1958 followed by another Germany picture.

The slides were stored in the basement and Grandpa's house in Farmington Hills had the same flooding problem as our home did when the electricity occasionally went off. The slides apparently survived several floods down there, but some did get wet and warped and would get caught in the machine during the slide shows, causing more interruptions. And when the show was over if you didn't let the fan run to cool off the projector bulb, the bulb would burn out, causing more delays in getting the next slide show underway.

Grandpa loved to take pictures, so I decided to follow in his footsteps. Ma gave me her old Brownie Hawkeye camera from the 1950s. It had a bulky flash attachment on one side. The single flash bulb had to be replaced for every picture. When the bulb flashed, it almost blinded you for a few seconds. My first roll of film was wasted as I kept opening the camera up, exposing the film to the light. I didn't know you couldn't do that!

TRAINS, PLANES AND A CELLO

*Pa and his brood
in another slide snapped by Grandpa*

Family slide shows were memorable, but once in a while we would go to a real movie! Occasionally Pa would pack us all up into the station wagon and take us to the drive-in theater. We would have to wait until it got dark for the show to start on the outdoor screen. The drive-in had a playground where we could wait for twilight to take its course. By the time the movie started, we usually were in the car in our pajamas ready to fall asleep as the previews appeared on the screen.

Ma liked the movies and would take us to the matinees at Livonia Mall. Pa rarely went with us, although once he took me to a wonderful nature movie about a bear entitled "Toklat." It was such an event they even sold a special souvenir booklet about the movie. I cherished that movie program for years and often wonder who produced that film as I never saw anything about it again.

THE LITTLE GROWNUP

Growing up in a one-language family must be pretty dull. Since English was not my parents' and grandparents' native language, their tongues sometimes were still stuck in the "old country." Ma says she was bewildered when she first arrived in Detroit from Germany and couldn't seem to find the street "Grashit" everyone spoke about. The true spelling G-R-A-T-I-O-T just didn't click. Ma soon conquered her German accent and could be mistaken for a native born American.

Pa on the other hand retained his European way of pronunciation. A ten-acre real estate parcel in Wolverine became a ten-acre "partial." If you were cold, you were "called." The letters "TH" together just were not pronounceable. Pa's "that's it" became "datset." "Give me" was "Gimmer."

If Oma didn't know the English word, she would just throw in the German equivalent. Her laundry room was her "Kammerl." Grandma's literal translation of the German invitation to come to dinner became the amusing "Everybody sit on the table!" Grandma liked to call me "sweetheart." With her saying it, it came out more like "zwee taat."

Grandpa's Croatian background just added to the polyglot merriment. We learned to call the end of the loaf of bread the "Krayack" and cursed rude drivers as "Prassas" just like he did. He told us it meant they were pigs.

Since Grandpa was actually my step grandpa, he wasn't German and didn't understand it. He still enjoyed going to Grandma's German social club functions though and occasionally listened to her German music.

Austrian singer Lolita had a hit record with a song she sung in German called "Seeman." It tells the story of a sailor and his homesickness. Grandpa must have heard the record a little too often and invented his own English translation. It simply went "sea man, sea man, go jump in a lake!"

Grandpa had a sense of humor perfectly made for a grandchild. His encore to "sea man" often was his "peanut song" with these lyrics: "A little peanut sat on a railroad track. Along came a train. Now he's nothing but peanut butter." I don't know if this was his own material or stolen from George Washington Carver, but I thought it was the most clever lyric I had every heard. Second, of course, to "sea man."

Grandpa's background was Yugoslavian and Detroit had a very large population of Croatian people. Once in a while Grandpa's traditions would be accented by attending one of the Croatian-American functions. Several times I got to attend a concert by the famous Tamburitzans. This group played little guitar or mandolin type instruments with very different melodies than the Germans would use for entertainment. Folk dancing would also be featured and for once I wasn't up on the stage but in the audience watching.

Baba, Grandpa's mother, continued to be an endearing lady in our lives. When I was very young she would sing to me in Croatian. Now she was getting up in years. She used a cane to get around, but her mind was still very sharp. One time Moni, Kurt and I were taken to Grandma and Grandpa's house where of course Baba also lived. They were going out somewhere with my parents. My siblings and I were given very important instructions by Grandma. "Watch over Baba and make sure she stays safe. That's your job until we come back." We took this very seriously and were quite proud when the adults came home and Baba was still doing well. Looking back of course we didn't realize the adults had reversed everything and Baba was actually babysitting us. Grandma just knew we wouldn't get into any trouble if she treated us as adults, giving us this important mission!

*Baba's birthday
with Ma presenting the birthday cake*

Baba's health was slowly deteriorating. One Easter, she asked me what I wanted. Her knitted blankets were to be admired, so I put that on my wish list. Her eyesight was failing and she worked on the project the best she could. When Easter came around, sure enough I had a red and blue blanket. It was only the size of a mat as that was all she could still accomplish and it had several holes and mistakes in it. I was so proud of that blanket it became my prized possession, beating out the chocolates and other sweets in my Easter basket.

TRAINS, PLANES AND A CELLO

Baba eventually had to go to a nursing home to live. I guess she just became too weak for Grandma and Grandpa to manage. We visited her in the nursing home from time to time and occasionally she would return home for short visits.

Any human being's first brush with death is very hard to grasp. In 1974 Baba died. It was strange to see the body of this once vibrant woman in her casket. On the way to the cemetery from the funeral home I rode with Oma and Opa. It was raining. Oma said, "The skies are crying because Baba is gone." We all cried that day.

After Baba died, Grandma and Grandpa went on a trip to Germany. While there, they bought a brand new bright yellow Volkswagen Beetle. They had it sent to Michigan. Grandma was still from the old school where women didn't drive. She never needed to drive in Detroit with regular bus service. Living in Farmington Hills didn't offer that option, so in her fifties she decided to get a driver's license for the first time. Grandpa took her to a vacant parking lot to practice and she passed the test. Grandma looked good in her VW Beetle and enjoyed the freedom of driving.

As already mentioned, Grandpa worked for Ford Motor Company. In those days driving a foreign car in Detroit wasn't looked on favorably. If Grandpa drove the VW to work, he was told to park in a spot at the end of the parking lot. Grandpa was pretty much loyal to his employer's products up to this point.

The first car I recall him having was a sleek light yellow Ford convertible. I knew some day I would want a convertible, too. It oozed class. Grandpa always said, "Everyone should own at least one in his lifetime." Later he traded it in for a Ford LTD. And it also evoked driver envy. The dark black interior and maroon exterior were the exact contrast to the previous convertible and I loved this car, too. I don't remember ever seeing another automobile like it.

Grandpa with me and his maroon LTD

Grandpa still enjoyed his Ford cars, but for some strange reason became enamored with an ugly Dodge Dart, which he bought used. This car was a boring metallic blue gray and its image was just as gray. Maybe it was out of spite that he insisted on driving his Dodge to the Ford plant every workday. If they didn't appreciate his VW, he would show them!

Ford Motor Company actually was very good to my Grandpa and our family. Every year they held a family picnic that we would attend. Plenty of food and games were featured. Ford also sponsored events such as a downtown Detroit visit to the Ice Capades show, which as I recall ended in a rather slippery drive home back to Southfield on a very blustery wintry night. I recall visiting the

TRAINS, PLANES AND A CELLO

Ford factory only once when we were picking out a sporty Ford racing jacket complete with Cobra and Ford logo patch on the side. They weren't free, but were quite inexpensive.

THE LITTLE GROWNUP

Toni Hinz and I peer out of her camper

CHAPTER ELEVEN
STEAK, BEAR MEAT AND LIVER

My parents and grandparents had many friends and some of them remain very endearing and memorable. Grandma's friend, Toni Hinz, could have passed for her sister. Toni was also from Germany and her husband Walter had been war comrades and friends with "Opa on the East Side." Toni and Walter lived in New Jersey, but usually once a year we would see them as they came to visit us in their motor home. Toni had a unique personality. She was a nervous and constantly chattering woman. Grandpa said she must have been vaccinated with a phonograph needle. She could drive you crazy with her constant talking, but she never did. She was someone we all admired and loved.

One evening my parents took us out to eat with Toni and Walter as our guests. We were dining at a beautiful lake front restaurant. From our table, we could see the water quietly shimmering in the light of the moon. The romantic mood of the place was interrupted, as Toni still didn't have her mind made up when the waitress took our orders. "What are you going to have? I don't know what I

THE LITTLE GROWNUP

want. What is this prime rib? Is anyone going to order prime rib? How about fish?" After seeing that everyone ordered steak, Toni decided to have one, too. This surprised Walter, who explained that she was never satisfied when she ordered steak. To that she replied, "I love steak. I'll eat it all, just wait and see."

I am a salad lover and so was Toni. We went to the salad bar and took gobs of things. They had everything from lettuce to mouthwatering cantaloupe and watermelon chunks. We took raisin bread, lettuce, fruit salad, and cottage cheese. Toni took the most. The waitress brought soup, and then she brought steaming hot bread. The French onion soup was flavored just right. Of course Toni had a hard time digging through the layer of cheese that covered the soup bowl. She would wrap the cheese around her spoon as if she were eating spaghetti. She said, "What kind of soup is this? I've never had anything like this before!"

The meal finally came. Even though I was pretty full from eating the appetizers, I managed to polish off my steak and baked potato. Everyone else at the table finished up, too – except for Toni. She played with her food, while she babbled on about how enormous the portions were. She would shift her steak from one end of the plate to the other without even cutting into it. She just wanted to give the impression that she was busy eating. She did manage to finish off most of her potato. Demanding a doggie bag, she then proceeded to put her uneaten meat and small loaf of white bread into the bag. When she attempted to put her potato in with the meat, Walter told her not to. She then explained, "I will put it in the camper. I do this all the time when we go out to eat. Tomorrow I will have a nice lunch."

STEAK. BEAR MEAT AND LIVER

At our house, she put the steak in our refrigerator. The next day she said she wasn't in the mood for steak. The day after that she wanted smoked fish. A week later she was still promising to eat the steak. Then she went home to New Jersey. We left the steak in the icebox for a while after that, just to remind us of the fun and sometimes embarrassing evening that we had spent with her.

Childhood crisis didn't happen very often, but Monika certainly added one memorable one. She wanted pierced ears as she wanted to wear earrings. Apparently her ears didn't take too well to the earrings and the new hole. She cried and cried over the pain. Finally she decided it was too much and she refused to wear the post earrings, which were necessary at the beginning to make sure the hole stayed open.

When the hole closed and she saw that she couldn't wear earrings, she cried and cried about that. She had to get her ears re-pierced and the pain started all over again and you guessed it, the crying. This is long before men wore earrings and all I could think of at the time was why would anyone go through all of that?

Mealtimes are interesting to recall. When I was very young, Ma enticed me to eat by covering up pictures of Donald Duck and his nephews on a colorful plastic plate. If I ate the food on the plate, they would appear. Grandpa used his "airplane feeding" method on all of us during our younger years. This involved coaxing us to eat things we didn't want by putting the food on a fork and sailing it around the table. As it aimed at various diners' mouths he would narrate, "The plane goes to Grandma, goes to Monika, goes to Hansi. No! It goes to Kurt!" At that point the fork would dive for Kurt's mouth and he better open or he might get stabbed with it. Usually we all had our mouths open, as the stunt was quite comical.

Ma and Pa sometimes used tricks to get us to eat as well, but they weren't as ingenious as Grandpa. They told us liver was steak. Apparently we believed them although I remember it didn't taste like the steak Oma made. Once Pa thought he would kid us and told us a real beef steak was bear meat. That was the end of that supper as far as we were concerned and we refused to eat. Pa was enraged, but as Ma told him, "That's what you get for lying to the kids!"

Pa wasn't exactly the gourmet eater of the family. His favorite was taking a piece of white bread, spreading it with butter, and then pouring a large helping of pure sugar on top. He also ate double smoked bacon from the German butcher shop, which looked like a big hunk of white whale blubber. Yuck! I did like the German style Chamberlain rye bread he put it on.

Ma says when she got married she wasn't much of a cook. I would beg to differ. There were family favorites, like hot waffles right out of her waffle iron filled with ice cream. Ma usually bought Neapolitan ice cream since it had chocolate, vanilla and strawberry in one package. I preferred chocolate. Other Irene Borger kitchen classics included "Cream Tuna Fish on Toast," which consisted of a can of tuna, cream of mushroom soup, and green peas served on toast points. Or how about "Swankie Frankies?" These were broiled hot dogs filled with cheese and wrapped in bacon. Lasagna usually graced a birthday dinner, with recipe taken directly from the Emmanuel Lutheran Church cookbook.

STEAK, BEAR MEAT AND LIVER

I was the easiest of the Borger food connoisseurs. I'd eat most anything. Kurt, on the other hand, was very difficult. More than once he refused to eat what was served and Pa threw a fit. "There are children starving in Romania who would love to have those vegetables!" "Well, mail it to them then," Kurt would exclaim, which didn't go over to well with Pa. Sometimes Kurt would be told, "You just sit there until you finish your plate." So Kurt would sit. And sit. And sit. Then he'd complain that the food was cold and he couldn't eat it anyway. "OK, then you can leave the table." He always won. And he always got his way. Most of the time he preferred a hamburger or hotdog.

On our birthdays it was a custom that we could pick out a restaurant and we'd all go out for dinner. Being the gourmet that I was, I inadvertently picked a restaurant that didn't offer any of Kurt's comfort food on the menu. We arrived at my chosen restaurant but soon had to leave to accommodate Kurt's palate.

Of course this drove Oma crazy as she always said she never coddled Kurt's appetite and he always ate anything she gave him. Grandpa and Grandma had a different approach. They invited me over to dine with them and didn't invite Kurt. This was a great honor for me. Grandma's chicken dinners were wonderful. Usually the chicken would be placed on a rotisserie on the outside barbeque grill. As it spun around it would be basted with lemon butter. I loved the chicken drumstick. Grandpa didn't appreciate but tolerated me stirring my cut up chicken in with the mashed potatoes, peas and carrots, red cabbage and gravy to make a glob of tasty hodgepodge to eat.

THE LITTLE GROWNUP

Grandpa wouldn't do that. He always had class. A candle burning on the table. A small glass of wine. Years later Grandpa told me he didn't like the dark meat and was glad it was my favorite. Grandpa had a sweet tooth. Grandma made some good desserts. Her cookies were a treat, but admittedly everyone's favorite dessert was Oma's homemade German torte.

In the pre-cholesterol worry days, this cake was high on everyone's wish list, with its almost pure butter frosting and wine or rum drenched cake inside. It had about a zillion layers to it and probably as many calories. A ten year old boy doesn't care about that. The adults of the time apparently didn't either, as the cake was quickly devoured at holidays and birthday parties.

Every family has some friction and ours had its share. The entire story is not too clear as everyone has different versions. When Pa arrived in the United States, he was already an adult. Oma and Opa sacrificed a lot to get him here. He lived with them when he arrived and as Oma tells it he wanted to do things his way, not hers. Hers was the right way, according to Oma of course. Pa was a grown man and obviously had other plans for his life. He wanted to do things his way. Pa and Oma had similar "my way or the highway" attitudes, and neither one is ever known to have budged much. Pa claims Oma and Opa didn't want him to marry Ma, but he did so anyway and moved in with Ma's father ("Opa on the East Side") before the wedding. By the time I arrived on the scene peace had been made, but the underlying friction would always be there and flare up from time to time.

STEAK. BEAR MEAT AND LIVER

This sometimes meant poor me was used as a pawn in peace negotiations. Once in a while during these family feuds we didn't see much of Oma and Opa. Naturally I wanted to see them, but no effort was made to reconcile. I recall throwing a successful temper tantrum after church one week when I saw them there. Oma also told the story that one time I was staying at Grandma and Grandpa's house for the weekend. I mentioned that I wanted to see Oma and Opa. This happened during another family argument between Pa and Oma and Opa. Grandpa drove me to Oma and Opa's and as Oma recalls, "You gave me a big hug and everybody was crying." Oma said she immediately took me to the store and bought me some pajamas and I stayed overnight with her and Opa. Grandpa picked me up the next day.

Grandpa apparently wasn't totally immune from Pa's wrath either. On another occasion we were at Grandpa's house visiting, when Pa apparently spanked me for something I didn't do. Grandpa told him he didn't want his grandchildren being spanked in his home. Pa didn't like that and once again the visits were on hold for a while. This couldn't have lasted very long as Grandpa's temper was certainly not on the same level as Pa's or Oma's.

Just like any parents, Pa and Ma did the best they could. Pa wasn't one for coddling his children and tended more towards impatience. He ruled the family and in his mind was always right. If we didn't do what we were told, we would get a spanking. Most of the time his hollering instilled more fear in us than the spankings. If we wanted something, we usually had a better chance by asking Ma. Her usual reply to most anything we

THE LITTLE GROWNUP

wanted permission for was the non-committing, "We'll see."

Holidays are special times for children. Hosting the dinner was usually rotated between my parents and grandparents so they all weren't burdened by the stress. Easter was a major holiday that included church, Easter baskets full of candy, and a family feast. The dinner would include the annual Easter egg fight. This involved us all choosing partners and cracking the ends of the colored hard-boiled Easter eggs against the end of our opponent's egg. The person with the last uncracked end of the egg would be proclaimed the winner of the year.

After dinner we would usually join the adults for a card game Grandpa called "help your neighbor." I think he substituted the word "help" for something else, as you exchanged cards with the person next to you, usually to their disadvantage. Grandpa would usually play a chess game with Pa, Opa or Dorothy.

Aunt Dorothy and Grandpa ponder chess while Winnie ponders a tennis ball

STEAK, BEAR MEAT AND LIVER

Halloween was usually spent dressing up and going trick or treating around the neighborhood. Ma had made a leopard outfit and it was passed down through the years to us all. I also remember going as a ghost and Frankenstein. Perhaps the most memorable store bought mask was a clown that Kurt had one year. Unfortunately the eyes of this clown mask were quite tiny and when he couldn't see out of them he cried and threw a fit. I think Ma had to improvise something at the last minute.

Leopard Monika and her brothers

Several years we got to go trick or treating twice. Grandma and Grandpa's neighborhood didn't always celebrate Halloween on October 31st, so we would go visit them to get in some extra candy. Grandma always made a homemade pumpkin pie with fresh whipping cream, which we enjoyed before the neighborhood begging. We always did well in their neighborhood, as the houses in Farmington Hills were closer together and the people a bit more generous.

Thanksgiving Day was always very traditional with the turkey and stuffing and trimmings. The turkey was usually purchased at a special turkey

THE LITTLE GROWNUP

farm in Novi, Michigan. When we visited the farm, the turkeys were still alive and you could pick the one you wanted. I'm not sure if anyone could actually prove that the one you picked from the pen was the actual one you eventually bought ready for the oven. We usually watched the Hudson's Thanksgiving Day Parade from downtown Detroit on television while the bird roasted in the oven. That parade featured the biggest United States flag in the world hanging from the downtown Hudson's store.

Christmas has always been my favorite holiday. We usually went to a tree farm and watched Pa cut our own Christmas tree down, after we carefully selected it. Grandpa usually bought his from Scott's Nursery. Opa and Oma had the same artificial tree every year, as the needles of a live tree would not have fit in with Oma's idea of a clean house. Every year we would invariably snap a couple of pictures in front of our various Christmas trees. I wondered why we always took a picture of Oma's tree, as it looked exactly the same every year!

*Oma and Grandma
compare their Christmas gifts*

STEAK, BEAR MEAT AND LIVER

Christmas music played in our house all season long. Ma had a selection of records that she played annually. The Holiday Sing Along with Mitch Miller was one of our favorites and we knew the words to every song as we sang along.

One year my friend Bill and I went out Christmas caroling. I took my accordion along in a wagon as we pulled it down the street and visited the various neighbors. They all were quite enchanted by us and we got Christmas cookies and plenty of cash. We were making so much money we even went to the neighboring subdivision to try our luck and sure enough made even more money. Pa didn't think it was fair that we split the money fifty-fifty as I did more work, both singing and playing the accordion. I didn't care. It was fun.

Being the adored grandchildren that we were, we were usually showered with Christmas gifts. We provided a list to Santa Claus via Ma and Pa of what we wanted. Usually the list was heavily influenced by the television ads we saw. One year I insisted on getting a Johnny Bench baseball practicing device. Johnny Bench was a baseball player and suddenly became my idol. I don't know why. I wasn't really into baseball, but apparently the incessant ads on television told me I needed to have his batting practice gismo. I got it. It held my interest for a short while and then was relegated to the garage. For a short time I also collected baseball cards. I have no idea why.

Grandma usually bought us clothes for Christmas, as she wanted us to look nice. Once in a while she could be influenced to buy toys as well. Lucille Ball was advertising a game called "Pivot Golf" on television. I loved Lucy and of course had to have this piece of plastic junk as

THE LITTLE GROWNUP

well. Grandma bought it for me. I knew long before Christmas that it was mine. She had placed the gifts under the tree and wrapped them in such thin tissue paper that I could see the bold print on the box and Lucy's smiling face on it! When the big day came, the game didn't even work right. The plastic golfer didn't work. We had to order a replacement by mail. By that time interest in this latest fad had waned to nothing.

One memorable gift I asked for and received was a set of books entitled "Hiking the Appalachian Trail." This fascinating two-volume tome kept my interest for months as I read the intriguing stories of people who had hiked this 2175-mile trail that runs from Maine to Georgia. I then decided I would become a hiker as well and made plans to start buying everything from a mini stove to sleeping bag to backpack. I can honestly say that to this day I have never done any backpacking, although the armchair traveler in me still thinks that hiking that trail would be a grand and glorious experience.

Earlier I mentioned how talented Opa was with wood in his workshop. Pa had great talent in this area as well. He built homes, cabinets, and worked in the automotive industry as a model maker. Of course Pa and Opa had high hopes for me following in their woodworking genes. Unfortunately these genes weren't passed on in high enough potency.

Eric, my friend down the road, already was a whiz kid at a jigsaw and had even made me a picture of a raccoon. My case was hopeless. One year for Christmas I got a complete wooden workbench especially made just for me. It had little drawers and hooks for all of the tools, which were included. I could have sawed and planed wood to my heart's delight. My heart wasn't too interested however and my hands weren't coordinated enough to do it either. I found out I'd much rather play my mini electric organ I also had received that Christmas. Soon the old tunes like "Dark Eyes" and "Sidewalks of New York" blared through the house while the workbench sat in the basement looking forlorn.

Pa and Opa didn't give up that easily. The next year I got a wood burning kit. Not even Eric had something like that. It actually was quite a dangerous item for a boy. This was an electric thing you plugged in. The tip would get so hot it smoked. You used it like a pen to carve into wood. I tried it, but either it didn't hold my interest or I got burned too many times trying to use it properly.

Instead I focused my attention on another gift, the "Shrunken Head Apple Sculpture Kit" that Vincent Price advertised on television. This bizarre bit of kiddy marketing genius had children all over America carving up apples and hanging them near light bulbs to dry out. The "Shrunken Head Apple Sculpture Kit" wasn't as practical as anything Opa or Pa could have taught me, but it did make some very odd looking dried apples that no one needed, including me. Pa never gave up on me learning some of his ways of working with tools, but my eyes would just glaze over at the thought of attempting to do anything so foreign to me.

Vacation for a family of five can be expensive. Ma and Pa had already discovered the world of camping in Wolverine, but that was getting a bit old hat. Several other destinations were on the

THE LITTLE GROWNUP

agenda. One year we headed to Gatlinburg, Tennessee and stayed at Yogi Bear's Jellystone Park. This campground was a marketing success since every kid in America wanted to stay in a park related to the famous cartoon character Yogi Bear, which we all grew up watching. The park had many activities for children including hayrides and arts and crafts.

"Yogi" was there, too. Since the real Yogi was an animated cartoon, this was not an easy task to accomplish. An actor wearing a huge Yogi outfit and head made an appearance. The observant Borger kids could see the actor's face behind the screen in Yogi's huge mouth. "Why do you have a screen on your mouth, Yogi?" we asked. "That's no screen!" said the quick thinking Yogi. "That's chocolate cake!" Yogi's park was a franchise and we stayed at his park in Traverse City, Michigan, too. We didn't see Yogi there though. Apparently he stayed in Gatlinburg.

On the way home from Tennessee Pa got a bit sidetracked and stopped to ask directions. He asked someone at a gas station which way we needed to go to get back to Michigan. The Tennessee backwoods apparently hadn't progressed too far by the early 1970s as the man replied with puzzlement, "Michigan? Never heard of it!"

Another camping adventure took us across the Mackinac Bridge for a journey through Michigan's Upper Peninsula. People who live there call it "God's Country" and it was easy to see why. Miles and miles of roadway with nothing but nature as far as you can see. Once we got over the Mackinac Bridge we climbed Castle Rock and enjoyed the magnificent view. Pa found a little store that sold smoked fish and we enjoyed that

STEAK, BEAR MEAT AND LIVER

treat. We stayed at the state parks along the way, which were always tops.

An awesome boat ride along the coast of Lake Superior let us tour the Pictured Rocks National Lakeshore. Lake Superior had the coldest water I had ever felt. I went swimming in it for a short dip and my bones were numb! I took a few stones from the lake, as they were some of the most interesting and colorful ones that I have ever seen. We drove on to Copper Harbor, way up in the tip of the Upper Peninsula. We visited the fort and drove on the picturesque Brockway Mountain Drive. We toured a nearby copper mine and I bought a copper ingot.

The Porcupine Mountains had some of the most beautiful Michigan scenery ever. Unfortunately outside activity was not going to happen there for us as the black flies and other bugs rivaled my earlier camping trip to Rambler's Roost. At one of the state parks I played my accordion for the fellow campers who seemed to be enjoying it. I was sheltered from the bugs by a tent-like mosquito netting. As I ended one of my songs and everyone else was around a campfire, a park ranger appeared and wanted to know where the "noise" was coming from. He couldn't see me in my little tent. I guess that particular state park wasn't quite ready for the polka sounds of Hans.

Fellow campers always seem to bond well and we met the most delightful couple, Carl and Ruby Reed. As we continued on our trip, we eventually camped out at their home near Iron Mountain for several days. The hospitality of the Reeds grew into a longstanding friendship. While we were in Iron Mountain we took in the must see tourist trap, an iron mine. Other highlights of the trip through the Upper Peninsula included visiting the ghost town of Fayette and making the full circle back to the campground almost in view of the Mackinac Bridge itself.

Every child should have a pet and we certainly ran the gamut. I've already told you about my pursuit of a pet raccoon and aquarium and fish-eating frog. Through the years I also had a pet turtle, gerbil named "Maude," guinea pig named "Hogan" and several labrador retrievers. Monika was the animal lover in the family and she also had a rabbit hutch outside. I don't know what the big attraction of rabbits was as all they seemed to do was lay stinky little pellets that had to be cleaned up, but Monika enjoyed them. Monika and Kurt also had pet mice that would jump up to the top of their cages trying to get out. They would hit their heads so hard they would start bleeding, but they never gave up.

Hogan the guinea pig joins me on the front lawn

Monika also had a pet anole, a kind of chameleon lizard. It was part of a school science experiment and after the experiment was over, she brought it home. She named it "Lazy" and Lazy

STEAK, BEAR MEAT AND LIVER

basically just sat in a plastic shoebox sized cage. It didn't really do anything. Its main diet was flies.

Of course in the summertime that is no problem, but in the wintertime in Michigan flies are rather rare. Moni would get quite upset and cried, as Lazy's skeletal bones would show. He wasn't eating. She would dangle hamburger from a string trying to get the lizard to eat it. Somehow Lazy lived for quite a long time and survived the winter.

Moni wanted a companion for Lazy. At that time you could order these lizards through the mail. When the first shipment arrived, the lizard was dead. The replacement box did have a live animal, but it was so eager to get out of its confinement, it quickly leapt out of the box and behind the bookcase. It took quite a while to retrieve it. The long trip from Florida must not have been too relaxing, as it didn't live very long. At least we didn't have to do the dangling hamburger meat in January again for Lazy's companion, too. So much for Moni's memorable chameleons.

Grandma and Grandpa had perhaps the most adored pet of the family, a cockapoo mutt named Winnie. Winnie slept in a little dog basket under Grandpa's desk in the kitchen. Winnie was always happy to see us. If the doorbell rang, she'd dash from her basket to the doorway waiting to see who would be behind the front door. She loved attention. People's stories about their dogs can be rather boring, but Winnie could provide enough material for a movie. If Grandma and Grandpa left her at home alone, they would return to find the pillows from the couch strewn all over the floor. Winnie would show her wrath at being left behind! She also climbed on the kitchen table and would leave things in disarray.

THE LITTLE GROWNUP

Of course when anyone was home she was the perfect angel. She even ventured going down the dark steps into the basement to "do her business" if no one let her out. Winnie would invariably try to beg a few scraps out of anyone dining at the table. No one could resist. When Grandma had enough begging, she would holler "Los! In the basket! Los!" Using the German word "los," which means "get moving," let Winnie know Grandma meant business. Winnie would quickly retreat to the basket.

Winnie never liked going to the dog groomers, a place called Dog Gone Acres. She usually liked going for a ride in the car, but somehow she knew exactly when the trip was going to take her to the doggie beauty shop. She would cower and shiver like she was about to face an execution. She always survived the trip though, and the folks at Dog Gone Acres would always put a little bow on their sheared client, making her look like quite the princess. Winnie was a true member of the family and sometimes I think she was a lot smarter than many of the people I've known!

CHAPTER TWELVE
GOODBYE CITY LIFE

It was time for the seventh grade. Time for a new school. Levey Junior High was just a few minutes away from our house, so close in fact that I got permission to walk home for lunch. This not only broke up the school day but also let me watch part of my beloved "The Lucy Show" before going back for the afternoon. Levey was a whole new world compared to the laid back Eisenhower Elementary. Now we had so many books we needed lockers, two students to a locker. I got a special dispensation to share my locker with Debbie as we were such good friends. Normally they wouldn't allow a guy and girl to share a locker together!

The Levey teachers were quite memorable. Geography teacher Mr. Wolfe played a radio in class while we were taking tests. The gym teacher, whose name escapes me, didn't seem to do much of anything except tell his assistants what to do for him. By this time my interest in "physical education" was about gone. I was quite tall, which may have worked for basketball if I had the interest. The rest of the games seemed either too boring to me or too difficult for my uncoordinated gangly body to enjoy. With the teen years around the corner, I was very attuned to my physical appearance. By now my teeth required braces, which at that time meant wearing headgear and a mouth full of shiny metal.

I had friends but sometimes it was easier to enjoy a book. My love for reading and words had become evident in elementary school and I found a wonderful English class at Levey taught by a wonderful teacher. English enrichment was a step above Levey's regular English classes. It was taught by Rosemary Sargent, a very endearing lady who not only pushed us to read, but also increased our vocabulary. Mrs. Sargent helped us breeze through tedious studies of mapping English sentence structure. She gave us extra credit word games and puzzles. They were so hard I sometimes had our neighbor and puzzle expert Dorothy Blan working hard to help me crack them.

Mrs. Sargent's sense of humor was hilarious. Her grading scale for instance included what she called a "Sargent Circle E" which meant we didn't turn in the assignment! She used her own cussword "dern". I experienced many teachers through the years, but Mrs. S was "dern" special. Ma and Pa were so impressed they even had her and her husband over for dinner.

Mrs. Sargent encouraged the creative outlet Debbie and I had found in our tape-recorded "radio programs." Soon we even recorded special programs for her, including a slide show featuring Debbie, my sister and me as actors! Of course Monika got into the act since she was an experienced actress from all of the previous tape recordings she and I had made. It was a lot of fun and even now I can listen in on my childhood whenever I want through those old "programs."

from a slideshow skit for Mrs. Sargent

In later years we stayed in touch. Mrs. Sargent sent me books to read, and she and her husband even took Debbie and me on their yacht up the Detroit River. Sailing past the downtown skyline was quite impressive. I would only spend one year at Levey before our family was uprooted out of Southfield.

Pa was getting tired of working for someone else and wanted to live the American dream of owning his own business. Our vacation experiences in Wolverine had left him wanting less of the city life and more of the country. Around 1976 he got serious about this new idea. He looked at everything from convenience stores to gas stations. He eventually chose a combination restaurant, 14-unit motel, and campground in Roscommon, Michigan called the Tee Pee.

I don't think we had ever even been to Roscommon as we breezed our way up I-75 another hour or so north to Wolverine. Ma had her pre-marriage office experience and could easily take over book keeping. But what did a model maker and former house builder know about running a restaurant and motel? That didn't seem to matter as his dream house in Southfield was sold and we all packed up and headed to our new life in Roscommon. It wouldn't be easy leaving all my friends behind, but we were excited about this new venture.

Moni, Kurt and I were still young enough at this point that we couldn't offer much help in the business except maybe washing dishes in the restaurant. It was exciting to say "my parents own a restaurant," but it also marked the end of a lot of their free time to spend with us, as the new endeavor required more and more of their wits and attention.

Oma and Opa spent some time visiting us in our new surroundings. Oma even made some of her family favorite German torte cakes to sell in the restaurant. Unfortunately the northern Michigan clientele was more interested in a piece of apple pie or a hamburger than a new delicacy and that effort failed. I had hoped Oma would become famous worldwide with her cakes, just like Betty Crocker or Sara Lee. At least I had a supply of torte to eat at my fancy. Grandma and Grandpa also made a trip or two to Roscommon. It wasn't easy for Grandma to not have her daughter ten minutes away anymore.

Unfortunately not long after the restaurant and motel venture materialized, a major family tragedy happened. Grandma had been suffering from headaches for several months. She was only 57 and had always been healthy. The doctors couldn't seem to find out what was wrong. She had booked a trip to Germany to visit her aging mother and decided to still go despite her increasing pain. When she came back she was finally diagnosed. Grandma had a brain tumor and needed surgery to remove it.

I still recall her hosting a small dinner party prior to her operation. She put on a good face and seemed optimistic. Everyone hoped and prayed for the best. Looking back I don't know if the doctors knew how bad the outcome would be or if they just didn't tell her. She never came home.
Timing didn't help either, as Ma and Pa were tied up with their new business and couldn't spend days shuttling back and forth to visit her in Beaumont Hospital near Detroit. Grandpa coped the best he could but he was still committed to working at Ford's. He was overwhelmed by what was happening. The bulk of the visits seemed to fall on Oma, who made almost daily trips to make sure Grandma ate and got the care she needed.
Poor Grandma went through hell and it was an eye opening experience for an early teen like me to witness. Ma and Pa couldn't always get there, but I took the long Greyhound bus back south as it snaked through various cities and towns, before reaching Detroit. Grandma had been shaved bald and her skull was cut open where the tumor had been removed. Some visits she would be her old self, but other times she didn't even recognize me as I wheeled her around the hospital in a wheelchair or put lotion on her legs.
We tried to bolster her depression by bringing Winnie to the hospital. The dog couldn't be brought to the room, but we brought Winnie outside the hospital and Grandma looked at her through the window several stories up. The tumor couldn't totally be removed, so radiation and chemotherapy treatments followed.

Grandma was deteriorating. Her immune system was failing. She needed a colostomy. She had shingles. She was in pain. Ma bought some vitamin powder to put in her food. Oma brought in some German malt beverages and teas. Nothing helped. She reverted to speaking German and the staff didn't understand her. She was in agonizing pain and her cries echoed through the halls.

Perhaps the saddest sight was when Grandma's own aging mother made the trip from Germany to see her daughter during her last days in a nursing home, where she was released when the hospital couldn't offer any hope. My great-grandmother had visited several years earlier, but this reunion was quite sad.

When Grandma died, the funeral home reconstructed her disease-ridden face with makeup and once again she almost looked lifelike with her coiffed hair and beautiful dress. It was all very surreal to me, right down to the golden letters "Martha Margetich" on the sign outside of the funeral parlor room where her body was on display.

After the burial, Grandpa had a luncheon reception at his home. Toni and Walter Hinz made the long trip from New Jersey to attend Grandma's funeral. Toni had been Grandma's long time friend since their days in Germany. Toni and I retreated to one of the bedrooms to talk. We weren't up to socializing with the rest of the house. Toni told me that Grandma told her to watch over me when she was gone. We cried.

Somehow even eating the strawberry jam Grandma had canned before her illness brought back memories. Innocence was over. As with all deaths, the bereavement process has to be traversed.

GOODBYE CITY LIFE

The easygoing days of growing up were gone. The coming years would bring many exciting adventures, from my career in broadcasting to my marriage to my German-born wife Heike. Many of the people mentioned in this book would continue their importance in my life. But times were different. There is an old German folk song that translates as "the time of youth is beautiful. It will never come again."

As I get older it is very comforting to visit many of the memories shared with you here. At the beginning of this story, I mentioned Aunt Dorothy driving me past those old homes in Detroit. Perhaps now you too can almost see Grandma and Grandpa peeking out the window? And don't worry, Oma. We'll dust those fingerprints off of the piano!

www.ingramcontent.com/pod-product-compliance
Lightning Source LLC
Chambersburg PA
CBHW032002080426
42735CB00007B/486